The Nat[illegible] Series

Thr[illegible] the Year

Elizabeth Martin

Illustrated by Alan Harris

Series Editor Lionel Bender

Macdonald

This book was designed and produced
by The Oregon Press Ltd, Faraday House,
8-10 Charing Cross Road, London WC2H 0HG for
Macdonald & Co. (Publishers) Ltd, Maxwell House,
Worship Street, London EC2A 2EN

Series conceived, designed and edited by
Lionel Bender, 10 Chelmsford Square,
London NW10 3AR, assisted by Madeleine Bender

ISBN 0-356-09719-6

Printed and bound by William Collins Sons
& Co. Ltd, Glasgow

CONTENTS

How to use this book	*4*
Types of trees	*6*
How trees work	*7*
Clues and evidence	*10*
Tree distribution	*14*
Interpreting the evidence	*15*
Keys/Ready reference section	*16*
Species fact files	*26*
Practical section	*72*
Recommended sites	*78*
Further reading/Glossary	*79*
Index	*80*

How to use this book

Trees – through the year is designed as a practical guide for recognizing and positively identifying all the common trees of western Europe, both native and introduced, at all times of the year. It is divided into several sections, which lead from the search for clues and evidence and identification of types, or species, to active practical work on collecting and preserving specimens. It is hoped that this approach will encourage a positive interest in trees and an increased awareness of the important role they play in our landscape.

Types of trees, page 6.
This page shows you how to distinguish between trees and shrubs and outlines the main differences between the two main types of tree, conifers and broadleaved.

How trees work, pages 7-9.
This section describes the functions of the various parts of the tree that are used in identification in this book. It provides interesting background information that will help you to appreciate that trees are living organisms and should be treated with care. While most wild species can spare a few leaves, flowers or fruits, it is best to search first for twigs that have become detached from the tree. Never remove the bark from any tree – it has an important protective function.

Clues and evidence, pages 10-13.
An imaginary woodland scene is illustrated at different times of the year to show you what clues and evidence are available at various seasons and so enable you to identify the trees. The same sorts of evidence can be found in other habitats, such as parks, gardens, streets and plantations.

Tree distribution, page 14.
On this page are listed the trees likely to be found in habitats other than woodlands. All the trees mentioned here, and on the previous pages, are treated in detail in the later sections of the book.

Interpreting the evidence, page 15.
This section summarizes the information given in the *Clues and evidence* section and provides an introduction to the *Keys* and *Ready reference* sections that follow. Read this section carefully before you start searching for and identifying your clues.

Keys, pages 16-21.
These pages provide a simple but comprehensive means of identifying trees by means of their winter buds (*Key i*) and leaves (*Key ii*). The keys are easy to use and are fully illustrated.

Ready reference, pages 22-25.
In this section other kinds of evidence are presented in such a way that you can easily compare your specimen with those illustrated. Three groups of clues are considered: (i) *Crown and bark*; (ii) *Flowers*; (iii) *Fruits and cones*. Together with the keys, it should cover all the evidence you are likely to find.

Species fact files, pages 26-71.
This, the main section of the book, presents detailed information on 57 common species of trees. Each fact file fully describes and illustrates the whole tree, its bark, winter buds, leaves, flowers and fruit or cones. In addition, information is given on habitat, distribution and annual cycle of growth. The fact files therefore collect together all the clues and evidence relating to particular trees. They can be used in the field, in conjunction with the keys and ready reference sections, to confirm your identification, or in the home as a reference source.

Practical section, pages 72-77.
These pages give instructions on how to keep records of your findings, how to preserve leaves, flowers and other parts, and how to make plaster casts and scribble prints. Using the methods described, you will be able to compile your own fact files and build up collections of specimens.

Recommended sites, page 78.
On this page are listed a number of well-known sites in England, Wales, Scotland and Ireland where you can see fine specimens of trees, both in collections and in their natural surroundings.

Further reading, page 79.
The books listed in this section provide a more extensive coverage of European trees, including the less common species, than has been possible in this book.

Glossary, page 79.
Brief definitions are given of words used in the text that may be unfamiliar to you.

Index, page 80
Includes the common names of all trees dealt with in this book.

6 Types of trees

Trees are woody plants that can grow to a great size and age. A typical tree has a single main stem, the trunk, which divides into branches and then twigs bearing the leaves and flowers, the whole structure forming the crown of the tree. The trunk and branches have an outer covering of bark. Shrubs are smaller woody plants, often with several stems. Some shrubs grow to a tree form and size if conditions for growth are favourable; others always remain as shrubs. Unlike herbaceous plants, neither trees nor shrubs die down in winter – they are known as perennials.

Although trees tend to look alike, they do not form a single botanical group and are not closely related to each other. They may be divided into two broad groups, *conifers* and *broadleaved* trees. Within these groups trees are divided into different families, depending on how many characteristics they share.

It is fairly easy to distinguish between a conifer and a broadleaved tree. Most conifers tend to have a trunk that continues to the top of the tree, producing branches along its length; the leaves are typically narrow and usually evergreen; and the tree reproduces by means of cones. Most broadleaved trees have a trunk that divides into several main branches, which form the crown; their leaves are of various shapes but never as narrow as conifer leaves; and the tree reproduces by means of flowers and fruit. Broadleaved trees may be deciduous, shedding all their leaves each winter, or evergreen, shedding and replacing their leaves throughout the year so that they never have bare branches.

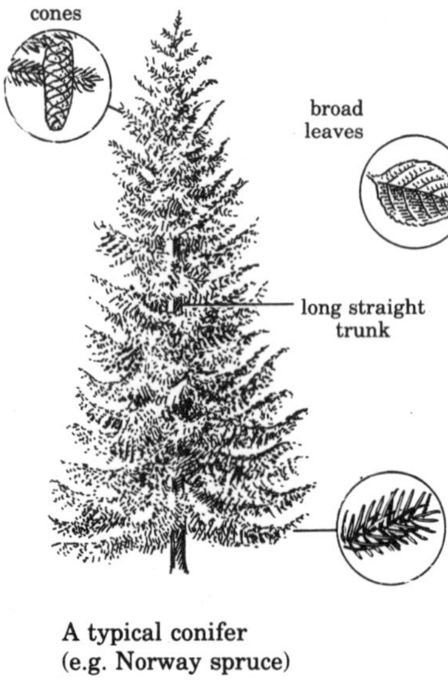

A typical conifer
(e.g. Norway spruce)

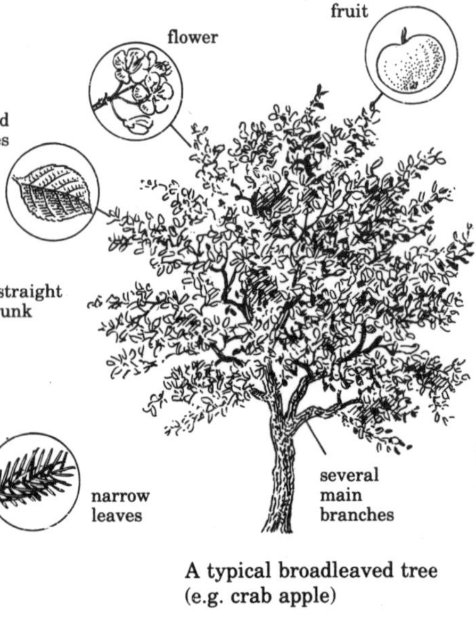

A typical broadleaved tree
(e.g. crab apple)

The parts of a tree that you will use to identify the species – leaves, bark, flowers and so on – all have different functions. They help the tree to feed, breathe, grow and reproduce.

Leaves The leaves of different trees vary in shape, size and texture, but they all contain a green substance called chlorophyll. This gives them their colour. Chlorophyll is essential for a process called photosynthesis, which takes place in the leaves. During photosynthesis, the chlorophyll absorbs light energy from the rays of the Sun. The energy is used to drive a chemical reaction in which carbon dioxide, absorbed by the leaves from the atmosphere, and water, drawn up from the soil, are converted into the sugar glucose. Glucose is used as food by the tree. Oxygen is also produced during this reaction and given off from the leaves. Leaves contain tiny pores over their surface through which the gases enter and leave.

The other main function of leaves is to provide a means by which water can leave the tree. Water is drawn up from the soil by the roots. What is not used for photosynthesis and other purposes passes out in the form of vapour through the pores in the leaves. The veins of a leaf contain two series of cells that carry substances to and from the leaf. Phloem cells carry the sugar made during photosynthesis from the leaf to all the other parts of the tree; xylem cells bring water from the roots to the leaf.

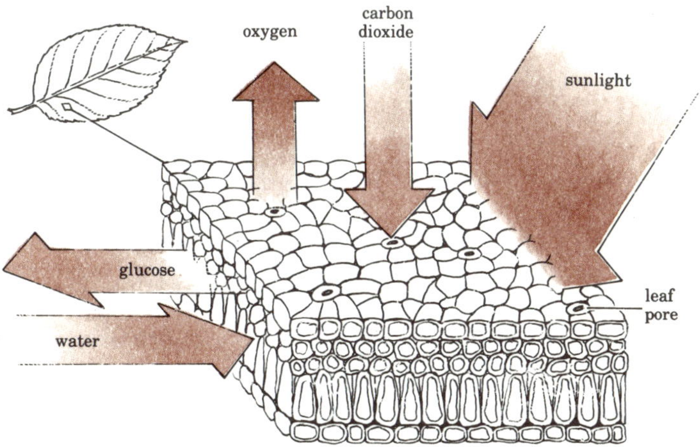

Photosynthesis in a leaf. The whole process can be summarized by an equation:

$$\text{carbon dioxide} + \text{water} \xrightarrow[\text{sunlight}]{\text{chlorophyll}} \text{glucose} + \text{oxygen}$$

How trees work ii

Trunk/wood The trunk of a tree consists of a thick wood core and a covering of bark. The wood consists of xylem cells, which carry water and take the form of tubes with thick walls. They are produced by rapid divisions of a layer of cells called the cambium. Each spring the cambium produces large numbers of big xylem cells, since this is the season of active growth when the tree needs most water. Smaller and fewer xylem cells are produced during the summer and autumn, and none at all in winter. As the years go by, each year's wood can be seen in the form of a ring, the oldest rings towards the centre of the trunk. Counting these rings will give the age of the tree. The cambium also produces phloem cells, which lie outside the wood, just beneath the bark.

Section of a tree trunk, showing four annual rings of wood

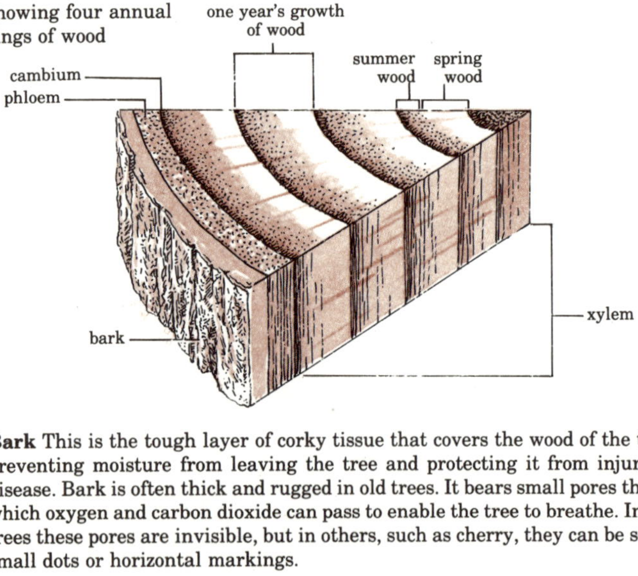

Bark This is the tough layer of corky tissue that covers the wood of the trunk, preventing moisture from leaving the tree and protecting it from injury and disease. Bark is often thick and rugged in old trees. It bears small pores through which oxygen and carbon dioxide can pass to enable the tree to breathe. In some trees these pores are invisible, but in others, such as cherry, they can be seen as small dots or horizontal markings.

Section of bark

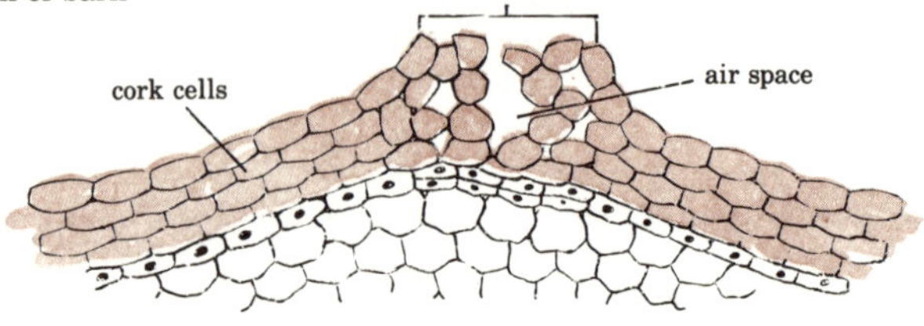

Winter buds In autumn, on broadleaved trees, buds are formed at the tips of the shoots. These buds remain on the tree during winter, after the leaves have fallen, and are very helpful in identifying the tree in this season. Within the buds are miniature shoots, leaves and flowers that will suddenly expand the following spring to produce the next season's foliage and flowers.

Flowers and fruit Flowers contain the reproductive organs of a broadleaved tree. Some species, such as hawthorn and magnolia, have conspicuous flowers with petals; others, such as oak, ash and hazel, produce many very small flowers that lack petals. The most important parts of the flower are the stamens and pistil, and all flowers have either or both of these. The stamens produce masses of yellow pollen, containing the male sex cells. This is deposited on the stigma of the pistil and fertilizes the female sex cells within the ovary. In petalled flowers the pollen is carried to the stigma by insects (such as bees), which are attracted by the colour and scent of the petals. In petalless flowers the pollen is usually transported by wind.

Once fertilized, the ovary of the flower develops into the fruit containing the seeds. The fruits of trees take many different forms, depending on how the seeds are dispersed. Cherry and apple, for example, have fleshy fruits, and oak and hazel have nuts; both forms of fruit are dispersed by animals taking them for food. Sycamore, ash and London plane, on the other hand, have dry fruits with wings or hairs to enable them to be carried away by the wind or water.

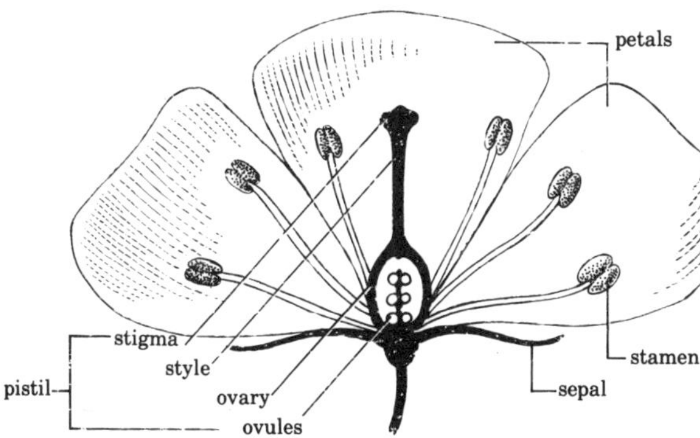

Section of a complete flower (with petals)

Cones The cones of coniferous trees, such as pine and larch, have the same function as the flowers of broadleaved trees. There are separate male and female cones. The males produce pollen, which fertilizes the female cone. After fertilization, the female cone becomes woody or leathery, its scales bearing seeds which are eventually shed. Cone seeds are dispersed mostly by animals.

Clues and evidence i – December-February

On the following four pages are shown the trees likely to be found in a typical mixed deciduous woodland. Each page depicts a different season. In the scene below it is winter and all the trees except the evergreen holly have bare branches. But evidence of identification may be seen in the winter buds and bark of some species, and towards the end of the winter catkins appear on early-flowering trees.

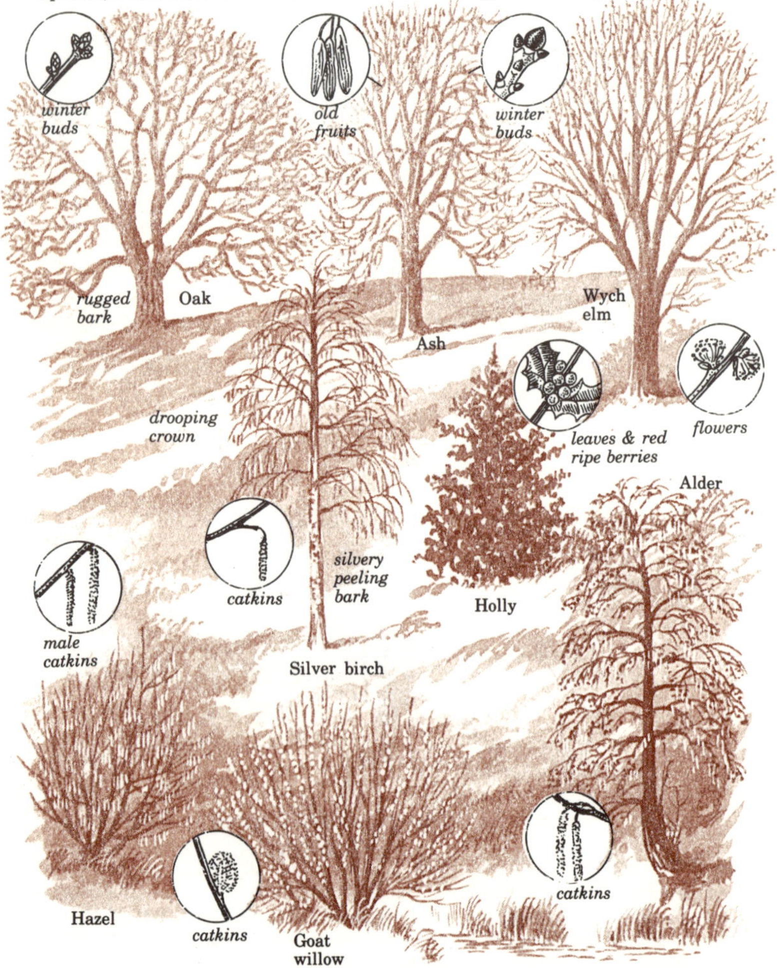

In spring the deciduous trees start coming into leaf and flowers appear. This is the best season for observing flowers, which usually have a short lifespan.

Clues and evidence iii – June-August

All the trees are in full leaf – summer is the best time of year for identifying trees. Flowers start to fade and many species begin to bear young fruits.

Autumn – the fruit season. The leaves of deciduous trees change colour and start to fall.

Tree distribution

On the preceding pages we have seen some of the trees that are likely to be found in a mixed deciduous wood.

Other native trees (and shrubs) found in woodland habitats are as follows:

- Scots pine
- Yew
- Hornbeam
- Beech
- Crab apple
- Whitebeam

Some smaller trees are typically found on the edges of such woods, in hedges and in scrub. These include:

- Wild cherry
- Pear
- Spindle tree
- Elder
- Juniper

Trees that often grow near water – on river and stream banks – include:

- Aspen
- Crack willow
- Weeping willow
- Goat willow
- Alder

Many of these native trees are often planted for ornament in parks, gardens and streets, along with introduced species. The latter include:

- Grand fir
- Cedar
- Larch
- Norway spruce
- Douglas fir
- Redwood
- Western hemlock
- Lawson's cypress
- Leyland cypress
- Monkey puzzle
- Lombardy poplar
- Walnut
- Sweet chestnut
- Holm oak
- Magnolia
- London plane
- Almond
- Laburnum
- False acacia
- Horse chestnut
- Common lime

Some conifers are also found in plantations and forests, where they are grown for their timber. These trees include:

- Grand fir
- Larch
- Norway spruce
- Douglas fir
- Western hemlock
- Corsican pine

In the woodland panoramas on pages 10-13 we have seen what kind of evidence is available for identifying trees at different times of the year. The most reliable features used for identification of broadleaved trees are winter buds and leaves, since one or other of these is present all the year round – winter buds from autumn until spring, leaves from spring to autumn. Most conifers are evergreen and can be identified at any time of the year by their leaves. On pages 16-21 are given keys for identifying trees by their winter buds (broadleaved species) and leaves (the key deals with both conifers and broadleaved species). These are very easy to use. Work through the list of options, each of which offers two choices. Reading across the line, when a number is indicated move on to this option in the list. When the name of a tree is given, this is the species to which the winter bud or leaf belongs. Turn to the page indicated for the fact file on that particular species, where you will find further details that will enable you to confirm your identification.

Many trees have other features by which they can be recognized. These are as follows:

crown and bark – all the year round

flowers (broadleaved trees) – late winter to early summer (depending on the species)

fruits or cones – autumn

These features are best used for confirming an identification based on winter buds and/or leaves; they should not be used as the sole evidence. On pages 22-25 these features are presented in the form of three ready reference sections. In each section the evidence is split into groups so that you can see at a glance if your specimen fits with any of those illustrated.

Below, as an example, we show how you can identify a beech tree at different times of the year using the keys and ready reference sections.

December-April

The tree has a long smooth grey trunk. Turn to **Ready reference i** – it might be beech.

Examine winter buds using **Key i** to confirm the identification of beech.

May-November

Examine leaves using **Key ii**. Confirm identification of beech by searching for:

flowers (May) – **Ready reference ii**

nuts (August-October) – **Ready reference iii**

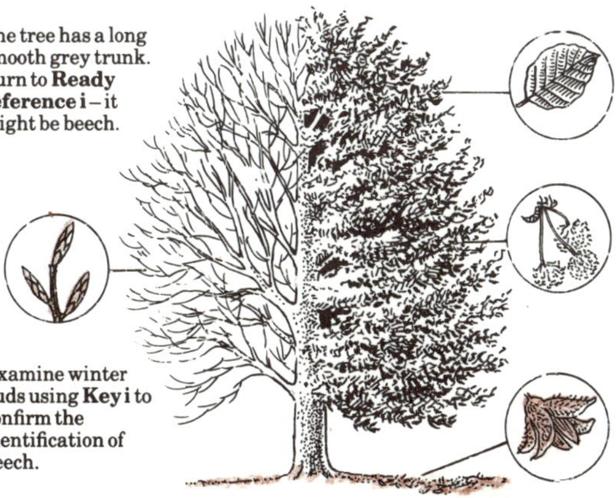

Key i – Winter buds and twigs

The key includes only those species with particularly characteristic and easily recognizable winter buds and twigs. Follow down the key until you come to the best description of your sample. Then refer to the corresponding page(s) for confirmation and further details.

1 Buds set in pairs  go to **2**

Buds set alternately  go to **6**

2 Buds lack scales 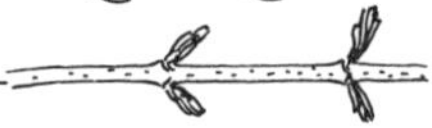 Elder p. 70

Buds have scales go to **3**

3 Buds green go to **4**
Buds brown or blackish go to **5**

4 Buds on green, square twigs  Spindle tree p. 66

Buds on greyish, rounded twigs  Sycamore p. 67

5 Buds black and small on grey twigs  Ash p. 71
Buds large and sticky; horseshoe-shaped leaf scars  Horse chestnut p. 68

6 Buds set on spiny twigs go to **7**
Twigs not spiny go to **8**

7 Spines set singly; buds very small  Hawthorn p. 55
Blackthorn p. 59
Spines in pairs  False acacia p. 64

8 Tip of twig bears cluster of buds; buds pale brown and very scaly  English oak p. 50
Buds not clustered at tip go to **9**

9 Buds more than 1.5 cm long go to **10**
Buds small go to **11**

10 Buds smooth, slender and red-brown  Beech p. 48
Rowan p. 62
Buds hairy  Soulange magnolia p. 53, Whitebeam p. 61

11 Buds hairy and grey-brown with pointed scales  Laburnum p. 63
Buds not hairy go to **12**

12 Buds on short stalks ——  —— Alder p. 44

Buds not on stalks —— go to **13**

13 Buds green; twigs warty ——  —— Silver birch p. 45

Buds brown or red-brown —— go to **14**

14 Twigs very stout;
buds squat and dark-brown  —— Walnut p. 43
Twigs slender —— go to **15**

15 Twigs hairy; buds round ——  —— Hazel p. 47

Twigs smooth —— go to **16**

16 Buds fringed with hairs ——  —— Crab apple p. 56

Buds not fringed with hairs —— go to **17**

17 Buds yellow-brown and
pressed to twig ——  —— Crack willow p. 41
Buds red-brown —— go to **18**

18 Buds slender and pointed ——  —— Hornbeam p. 46
Lombardy poplar p. 40
Buds oval —— go to **19**

19 Buds have single scale —— go to **20**
Buds have two or more scales —— go to **21**

20 Buds oval, pointed and
bright red ——  —— Goat willow p. 42
Buds have curved tip ——  —— London plane p. 54

21 Buds have two scales ——  —— Common lime p. 69

Buds have more than two scales —— go to **22**

22 Buds have many scales ——  —— Wild cherry p. 51

Buds have few scales ——  —— Sweet chestnut p. 49

In this key the leaves are divided into four groups.
A. **Needle- or scale-like leaves** – the leaves of conifers: usually present all year; always very narrow or small.
B. **Simple unlobed leaves** – the leafstalk bears a single leaf with a smooth or toothed margin.
C. **Simple lobed leaves** – the leafstalk bears a single leaf whose margin is indented by rounded or pointed lobes.
D. **Compound leaves** – the leafstalk bears a number of separate small leaves (leaflets).
Decide which group your leaf belongs to and work down the list of options for that group.

A. **Needle- or scale-like leaves**

1 Leaves narrow and needle-like – go to **2**
Leaves short and completely cover the twigs – go to **11**

2 Needles borne singly – go to **3**
Needles in groups of 2 or more – go to **8**

3 Needles grow from pegs all round twig and point forwards  – Norway spruce p. 30
Needles grow in two rows – go to **4**

4 Undersurface pale green; needles flattened  – Yew p. 37

Undersurface has 2 white bands – go to **5**

5 Needles are all the same length – go to **6**

Needles of various lengths (0.5-1.8 cm) and have rounded tips 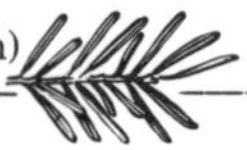 – Western hemlock p. 33

6 Needles on all the shoots – go to **7**

Needles on side shoots only; main shoots have scale leaves  – Coast redwood p. 34

7 Needles to 5 cm long  – Grand fir p. 27

Needles 2-2.5 cm long  – Douglas fir p. 32

8 Needles are long (7 cm or more) and borne in pairs  – Scots pine, Corsican pine p. 31
Needles less than 3 cm; not in pairs – go to **9**

9 Needles in whorls of 3  Juniper p. 36

Needles in tufts of 10 to 30 — go to **10**

10 Tufts grow from short spurs; needles soft and deciduous 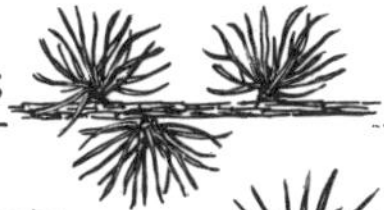 Larch p. 29

Tufts grow straight from shoots; needles hard and evergreen  Cedars p. 28

11 Leaves tiny and scale-like  Lawson's cypress, Leyland cypress p. 35

Leaves triangular and pointed  Monkey puzzle p. 38

B. **Simple unlobed leaves**

1 Leaves more than twice as long as broad — go to **2**
Leaves less than twice as long as broad — go to **6**

2 Leaves have smooth margins  Soulange magnolia p. 53

Leaves have toothed margins — go to **3**

3 Leaves more than 12 cm long; strongly toothed margins; prominent parallel veins 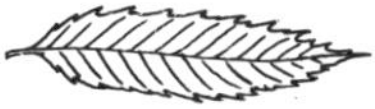 Sweet chestnut p. 49
Leaves less than 12 cm long — go to **4**

4 Leaves more than 3 times as long as wide; grey-green beneath  Crack willow p. 41
Leaves shorter than this — go to **5**

5 Leaves folded along midrib  Almond p. 58

Leaves not folded along midrib  Spindle tree p. 66

6 Leaves rounded — go to **7**
Leaves oval or triangular — go to **9**

7 Leaves have pointed tip — go to **8**
Leaves have indented or flattened tip and toothed margins  Alder p. 44

(Key continued over page)

8 Leaves have wavy margins and long leafstalks — Aspen p. 39

Leaves have toothed margins and are hairy — Hazel p. 47

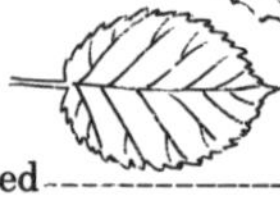

9 Leaves triangular or heart-shaped — go to **10**

Leaves oval and pointed — go to **12**

10 Leaves have lobed lopsided base — Common lime p. 69

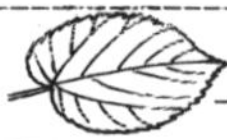

Leaves have symmetrical base — go to **11**

11 Leaves have a wide base and few teeth — Lombardy poplar p. 40

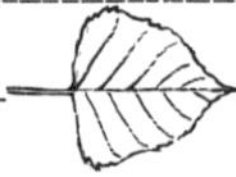

Leaves have a narrower base and many teeth — Silver birch p. 45

12 Leaves have smooth or wavy margins — go to **13**

Leaves have toothed margins — go to **15**

13 Leaves have smooth margins and are shiny and evergreen — Holm oak p. 51

Leaves have wavy margins — go to **14**

14 Leaves smooth, shiny, with parallel veins — Beech p. 48

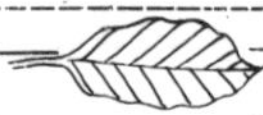

Leaves are crinkled and downy with red hairy stalks — Goat willow p. 42

15 Leaves have a lopsided base and prominent veins — Wych elm p. 52

Leaves have a symmetrical base — go to **16**

16 Undersurface white and downy — Whitebeam p. 62

Undersurface green — go to **17**

17 Leaves are finely toothed — go to **18**

Leaves are coarsely toothed — go to **19**

18 Leaves are glossy dark green with a long green stalk — Pear p. 60

Leaves are dull green with a short reddish stalk — Blackthorn p. 59

19 Leaves shiny on both surfaces with prominent parallel veins and a short (1 cm) stalk — Hornbeam p. 46

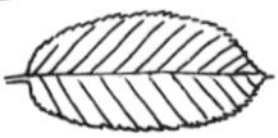

Leaves dull and downy beneath and have a longer (2-3.5 cm) stalk — go to **20**

20 Leaves 5-6 cm long — Crab apple p. 56

Leaves 10 cm long — Wild cherry p. 57

C. **Simple lobed leaves**

1 Leaves have rounded lobes — English oak, Sessile oak p. 50
Leaves have pointed lobes — go to **2**

2 Leaves 4 cm long or less; have 3 to 7 lobes — Hawthorn p. 55
Leaves more than 4 cm long — go to **3**

3 Lobes end in spines; leaves shiny and evergreen — Holm oak p. 51, Holly p. 65
Lobes do not end in spines — go to **4**

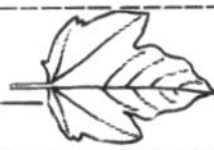

4 Undersurface white and hairy; leaves have 3 to 5 lobes — White poplar p. 39
Undersurface pale green; 5 lobes — go to **5**

5 Lobes have many teeth — Sycamore p. 67

Lobes have few teeth — London plane p. 54

D. **Compound leaves**

1 3 leaflets — Laburnum p. 63
More than 3 leaflets — go to **2**

2 Leaflets radiate from a single point — Horse chestnut p. 68
Leaflets arrange in pairs — go to **3**

3 Leaflets have smooth margins — go to **4**
Leaflets have tooth margins — go to **5**

4 7 to 9 dark green leaflets with pointed tips — Walnut p. 43

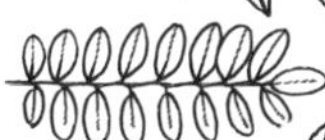

13 to 15 light green leaflets with rounded tips — False acacia p. 64

5 5 to 7 leaflets — Elder p. 70
More than 7 leaflets — go to **6**

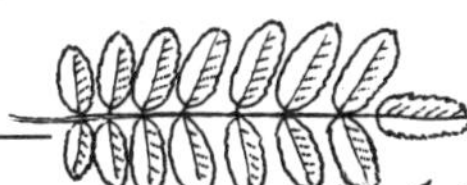

6 Leaflets 6 cm or less; margins smooth at base — Rowan p 61

Leaflets more than 6 cm; margins toothed all round — Ash p. 71

Deciduous trees A few species can be recognized in winter by their overall shape and/or bark.

Larch

Lombardy poplar

Weeping willow

Silver birch

Hornbeam

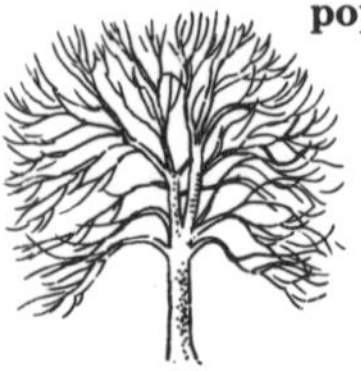
Beech

Sweet chestnut

English oak

London plane

Cherry

Laburnum

False acacia

Common lime

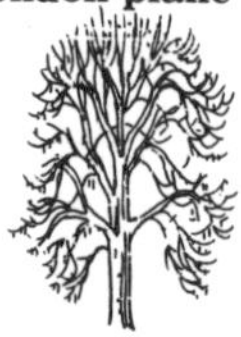
Ash

Evergreen conifers Most conifers have a characteristic shape and some have distinctive bark.

Grand fir

Cedar of Lebanon

Norway spruce

Scots pine

Douglas fir

Western hemlock

Redwood

Lawson's cypress

Juniper

Yew

Monkey puzzle

1. **Catkins** – small stalkless flowers arranged in clusters that are long and hang down from the twig. There are usually separate male (♂) and female (♀) catkins.
2. **Petalless flowers** – usually small and grow in clusters of various shapes.
3. **Complete flowers** – vary in size but all have conspicuous petals, stamens etc.

Decide to which group the flower you are examining belongs, note whether or not the tree is also bearing leaves, and compare it with the types shown below.

1. **Catkins**

a) Before leaves

Aspen

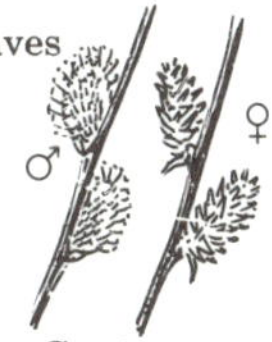

Goat willow

Alder

b) With leaves

Walnut

Oak

2. **Petalless flowers**

a) Before leaves

Wych elm

Ash

b) With leaves

Beech

London plane

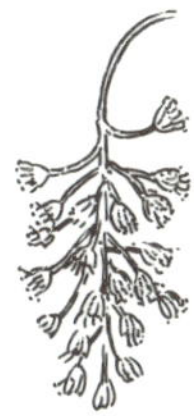

Sycamore

3. **Complete flowers**

a) Before leaves b) With leaves

Soulange magnolia

Hawthorn

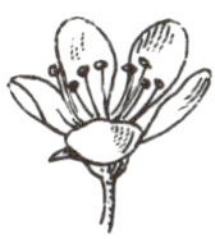

Crab apple

Flowering cherry

Rowan

Almond

Blackthorn

Holly

Laburnum

Horse chestnut

Lime

For the purpose of identifying trees, fruits and cones can be divided into the following six groups.

1. **Nuts** – hard, usually brown, fruits, often contained in a green leathery coat.
2. **Winged fruits** – these have flat wings or hairs that help them to be spread by wind. Winged fruits typically ripen from green to brown.
3. **Pods** – contain several seeds and split open when ripe; usually brown.
4. **Berries** – small round fruits, red or blue-black, growing singly or in clusters.
5. **Fleshy fruits** – larger than berries, of various colours and shapes.
6. **Cones** – woody or leathery structures made up of scales.

Note that these groups – and the definitions given above – are based on superficial appearance: they are intended only as aids to identification and do not reflect botanical relationships. For example, not all the fruits described as 'berries' are berries in the technical sense, and the 'cones' include the fruit of one broadleaved tree. Decide which group your fruit or cone belongs to and compare it with the types shown below. Species with similar fruits to those illustrated are given in brackets under the appropriate illustration.

1. **Nuts**

Walnut **Hazel** **Beech** **Sweet chestnut** **Oak** **Almond** **Horse chestnut**

2. **Winged fruits**

Hornbeam **Wych elm** **Sycamore** (Norway maple) **Lime** **Ash** **London plane** **Aspen**

3. **Pods**

4. **Berries**
a) Red

b) Blue-black

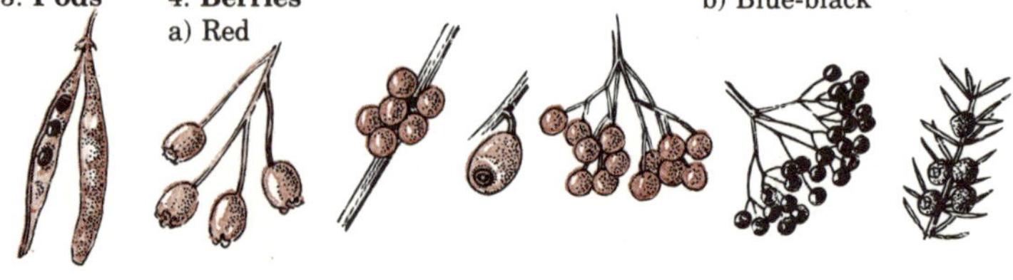

Laburnum (False acacia) **Hawthorn** **Holly** **Yew** **Rowan** (Whitebeam) **Elder** **Juniper**

5. Fleshy fruits

6. Cones

On the following pages, fifty-seven species of trees are described in detail. This selection includes those trees most commonly seen in N.W. Europe, both native species – those growing wild in their natural habitats – and introduced species – trees that are not of European origin but are widely planted in our streets, plantations and gardens. For reasons of space it does not include all common shrubs or those trees that are restricted to certain localities. Reference must be made to larger books, listed under Further Reading (p. 79), for details of these species.

The trees described in the Fact Files are grouped into their botanical families, starting with the conifers and working through gradually to the broadleaved trees. The name of the family is given at the top of each page. Within each family the species are arranged in alphabetical order of their botanical Latin names. Thus the family Rosaceae starts with **Hawthorn** *(Crataegus monogyna)* and ends with **Rowan** *(Sorbus aucuparia)*. Where the Latin name bears a × between the two compound names, this indicates that the tree is a hybrid. A hybrid is the result of the cross fertilization of two different species. It usually shows some of the characteristics of each of these.

Details provided The information in each Fact File is presented in a concise but clear form, with standard abbreviations for units (e.g. cm, m) and compass points (e.g. N, S, E and W). Two symbols – ♂ (male) and ♀ (female) – are used occasionally in illustrations to distinguish between male and female flowers or cones. The dimensions given for trees and their parts are usually the maximum found: there is often considerable variation between individual trees of a species, depending on their age and habitat. Similarly, the features of a tree are described in their typical form, and variation is common.

Each Fact File carries a *description* of the species, summarizing its general appearance and highlighting any prominent features by which it may be easily recognized. Characteristics of *bark, winter buds, leaves, flowers* and *fruit* or *cones* are also illustrated and described when these are important for identification. There are, in addition, notes under the following headings:

Habitat – indicating in which surroundings the tree is most likely to be found;
Range – stating its distribution, frequency of occurrence, and (for non-native species) country of origin;
Annual cycle – indicating the times of the year when the tree bears leaves (for deciduous species only), flowers and fruit, or cones. Winter buds are assumed to be present when the tree is not in leaf. For species whose cones take more than one year to mature, the cone cycle is given.

Certain species that are closely related to a main species and have many features in common with it are considered for convenience under the same heading. For example, the Fact File for Horse chestnut includes a brief description – together with illustrations – of the very similar Red horse chestnut.

PINACEAE

Leaves Flat needles, to 5 cm, arranged in two flat rows on shoots, bright-green above, marked with two white bands beneath. They smell of oranges when crushed.

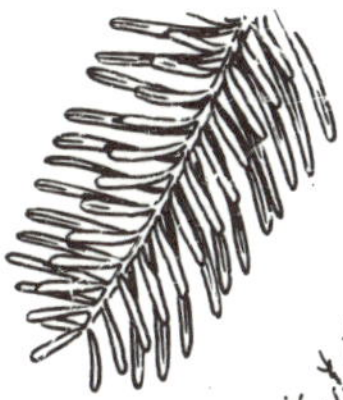

Male cones Oval and yellow, about 2 mm long, growing in clusters near the twig tips at the top of the tree.

♂

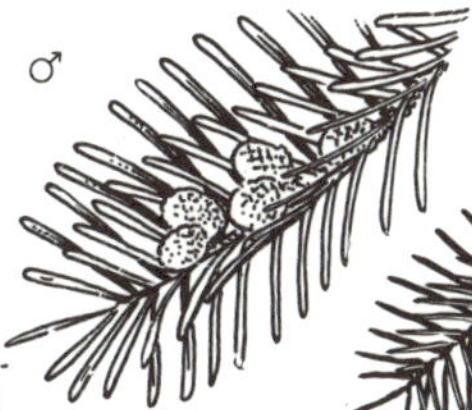

♀

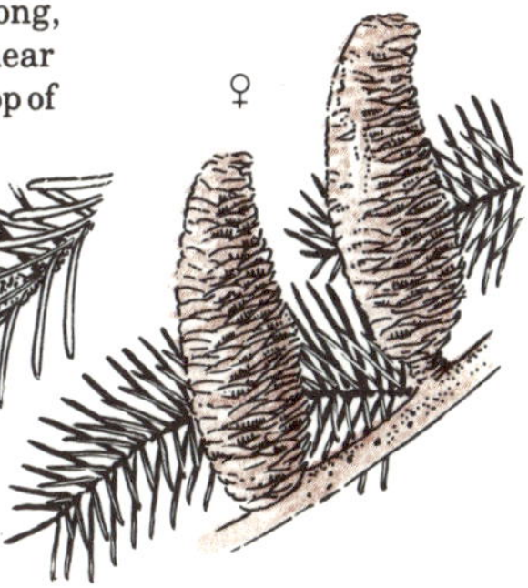

Female cones Green and pointed, ripening into upright cylindrical cones, 7-8 cm long, with smooth overlapping scales, at first bright green and finally red-brown. Rarely seen, as they are borne near the top of the tree and shed their scales when ripe, leaving a central spike.

Bark Brownish-grey with resin blisters when young; ages to dull purplish-grey, cracked into small square plates.

Description A tall, fast-growing, evergreen conifer, to 55 m, with a narrow conical crown and upturned branches.

Habitat Forests and plantations, where it is grown for timber, and large gardens, where it is planted for ornament.
Range Introduced from the W. coast of North America; widespread and common.
Annual cycle Male cones: April; female cones: April-October.

Cedar of Lebanon *Cedrus libani*

PINACEAE

Atlas cedar (*C. atlantica*) and **deodar** (*C. deodara*). Very similar to the cedar of Lebanon but can be recognized by their growth habits: the Atlas cedar has ascending branches; the deodar has branches with drooping tips and the branches themselves are often descending. The deodar also has longer needles (to 5 cm).

Description An evergreen conifer, to 40 m, with a wide-spreading, often flat-topped, crown and horizontal branches.

Female cones Green and bud-like, borne at the twig tips, maturing into large barrel-shaped cones to 12cm long. They break up on the trees releasing winged seeds.

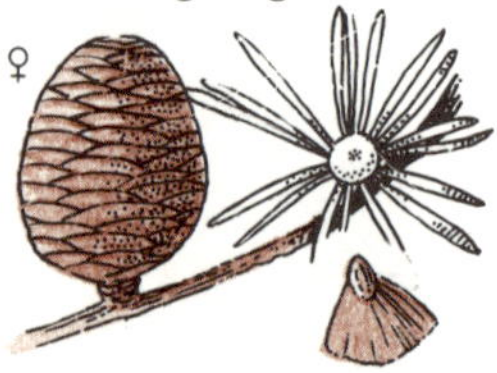

Male cones Greyish-green and conical, to 5 cm, becoming yellow with pollen in autumn.

Bark Smooth and grey when young, becoming brownish-grey and cracked into scaly plates with age.

Leaves Dark green needles, to 3cm, arranged singly on young twigs and in tufts of 10 to 20 on short spur shoots on older twigs. Some varieties have bluish-grey leaves.

Habitat Parks, gardens, churchyards and the grounds of large country estates, where it is grown for ornament.
Range Native to Syria and S.E. Turkey; widespread and common.
Annual cycle Male cones: June-November; female cones: November-November (take 2 years to ripen).

PINACEAE

Description A graceful deciduous conifer, to 40 m, with a conical crown of drooping branches that turn up at the tips. In winter the tree can be recognized by its shape and by its knobbly twigs, which hang down from the branches and often bear old cones.

Leaves Soft needles, 2-3 cm long, growing singly on young twigs and in tufts of 20 to 30 from knob-like spurs on older twigs. At first bright green, they become darker and finally golden-yellow in autumn.

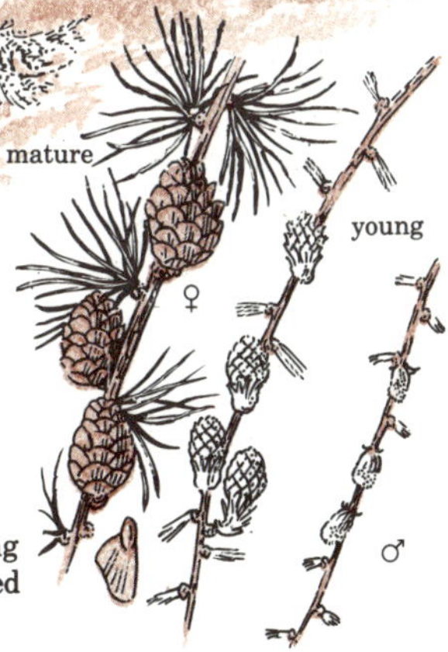

Female cones Red, flower-like rosettes of scales, becoming green and finally ripening into rounded brown cones, 2-4 cm long, with rounded scales. Old cones that have shed their seeds may remain on the tree for several years.

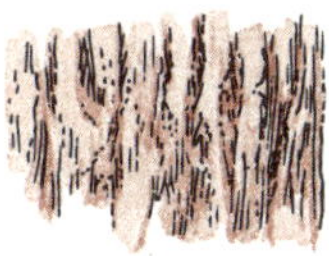

Bark Smooth and greyish-brown in young trees, becoming cracked and ridged with age.

Male cones Round and whitish, to 1cm, becoming yellow with pollen.

Habitat Plantations, where it is grown for timber, and parks, gardens and roadsides, where it is planted for ornament.
Range Introduced from C. Europe; common throughout N.W. Europe.
Annual cycle: Leaves: late March-late October; male cones: March-April; female cones: March-October.

Norway spruce *Picea abies*

PINACEAE

Leaves Stiff, pointed, dark green needles, to 2 cm, growing singly from small pegs all round the twigs. When they fall, the pegs remain, which makes the bare twigs feel knobbly.

Sitka spruce (*P. sitchensis*). Introduced from W. North America, it is similar to the Norway spruce but can be distinguished by its bluish-green leaves and smaller cones (to 8 cm), which have crinkly scales.

Bark Thin and rusty-brown, flaking into thin scales, becoming darker with age and cracked into small rounded plates.

Male cones Oval and crimson, to 1 cm, at tips of shoots, becoming yellow with pollen.

Female cones At first oval and crimson, borne upright near the tips of shoots; becoming green, turning down, and ripening into hanging, brown cylindrical cones, to 15cm, with smooth rounded scales.

Description An evergreen conifer, to 40 m, with a compact conical crown of horizontal branches. Young trees are familiar as Christmas trees.

Habitat Plantations, woods, shelter belts and gardens; grown mainly for timber and for use as Christmas trees.
Range Native to mountainous regions of N. and C. Europe; common in other parts of Europe.
Annual cycle Male cones: May; female cones: May-October.

Scots pine *Pinus sylvestris*

PINACEAE

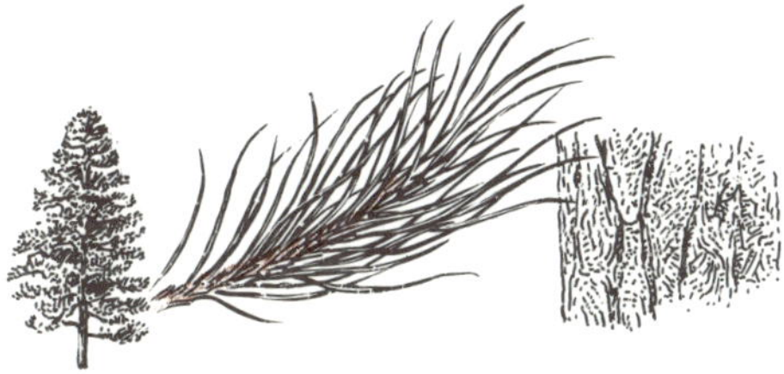

Leaves Blue-green needles, to 7 cm, growing in pairs on the twigs.

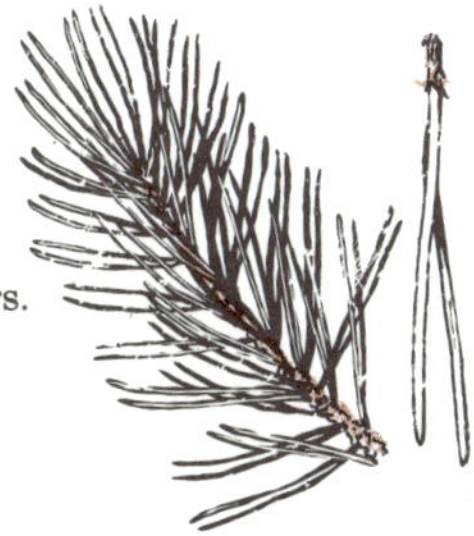

Corsican pine (*P. nigra* var. *maritima*). Native to Corsica and S. Italy, it is another common and widely planted pine. It differs from the Scots pine mainly in its thick, grey, ridged bark and its needles, which are longer (to 18 cm), grey-green, and grow in twisted pairs.

Female cones Rounded and pink, borne at tips of shoots, becoming bright green and turning down, finally ripening into grey-brown, oval pointed cones, 5-8 cm long. Old cones that have shed their seeds may remain on the tree but are also often found on the ground nearby.

Male cones Oval and yellow, to 1 cm, growing in clusters at base of shoots.

Bark Reddish-grey and cracked into plates on lower trunk; orange-brown or pink and scaly on upper trunk and branches.

Description An evergreen conifer, to 36 m, with a conical crown when young, becoming irregular and flat-topped, with sparse spreading branches and a long bare trunk, with age. Older trees can be easily recognized by their orange-brown upper trunk and branches.

Habitat Woods and plantations, where it is grown for timber, and parks and gardens, where it is planted for ornament.

Range Native to Scotland, N. and C. Europe, and W. Asia; common and widespread over the rest of Europe.

Annual cycle Male cones: May; female cones: May-October (take 2 years to ripen).

Douglas fir *Pseudotsuga menziesii*

PINACEAE

Description A tall, evergreen conifer, to 55 m, with a pyramid-shaped crown and horizontal or ascending branches. Despite its name, it is not a true fir, differing from the grand fir (p. 27) in its cones (see below).

Leaves Soft, flat needles, 2-2.5 cm long, arranged in two rows on the stems; green above and marked with two white bands underneath. They smell sweet when crushed.

Bark Smooth and grey-brown with resin blisters when young, becoming grey or purplish, thick and rough, with long, deep, orange-brown cracks, with age.

scale

Female cones Oval, and crimson, whitish or green, ripening to egg-shaped hanging cones, to 7.5 cm long, at first green and finally brown, with distinctive three-pointed bracts protruding from the scales.

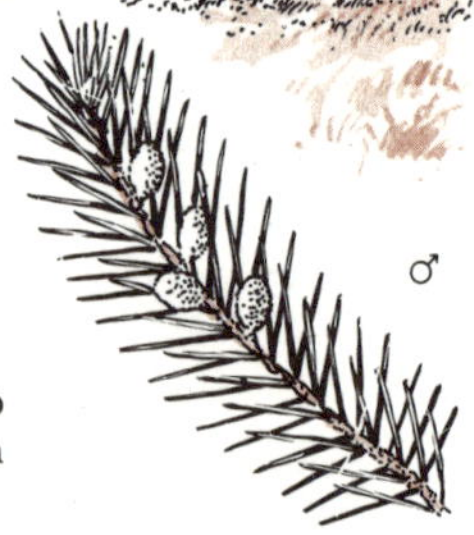

Male cones Oval and yellow, to 2 cm, borne near tips of shoots.

Habitat Gardens, where it is planted for ornament, and shelter belts and plantations, where it is grown for timber.
Range Introduced from W. North America; common and widespread in all parts of Europe.
Annual cycle Male cones: March-May; female cones: March-October.

PINACEAE

Male cones Rounded and crimson, to about 4 mm, becoming whitish-yellow with pollen. They grow in clusters among the needles.

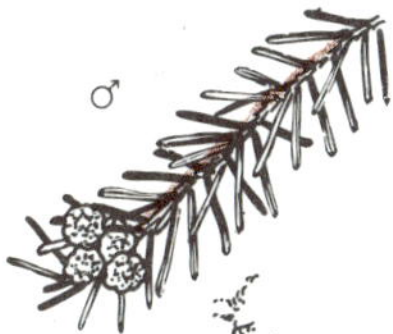

Leaves Flattened, round-tipped needles of various lengths (0.5-1.8 cm), growing in rows on the twigs. Shiny, dark green above and marked with two broad bluish-white bands beneath. They are strongly aromatic when crushed.

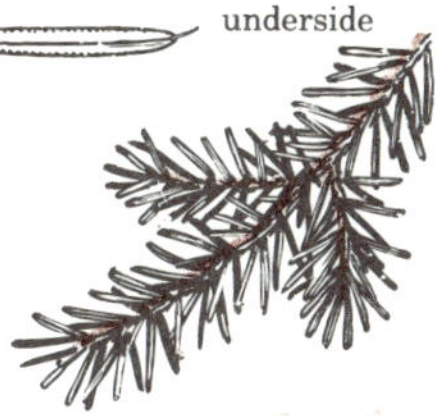

Female cones Oval and reddish-purple, to 6 mm, at the tips of shoots, ripening into hanging pointed egg-shaped cones, 2-3 cm long, at first purplish-green and finally brown, with smooth rounded scales. Old cones that have shed their seeds remain on the tree for some months.

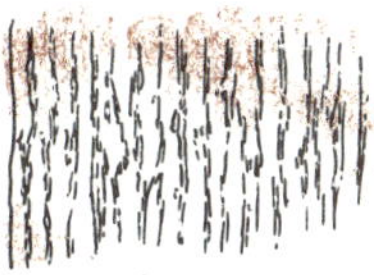

Bark Smooth and reddish-brown, becoming darker and thicker, with scaly ridges, in old trees.

Description A tall, graceful, evergreen conifer, to 45 m, with a narrow conical crown the tip of which droops downwards. This drooping leading shoot is a distinctive feature.

Habitat Plantations, where it is grown for timber, and gardens, where it is planted for ornament.
Range Introduced from W. North America; common in N.W. Europe.
Annual cycle Male cones: April-May; female cones: May-October.

Coast redwood *Sequoia sempervirens*

TAXODIACEAE

Female cones Small, rounded and green, at the tips of larger shoots, ripening into woody brown rounded cones, 2 cm long, with wrinkled scales. Old cones that have shed their seeds remain on the tree for some years.

Male cones Oval and whitish-yellow, 2 mm long, at the tips of small side shoots, becoming yellow with pollen.

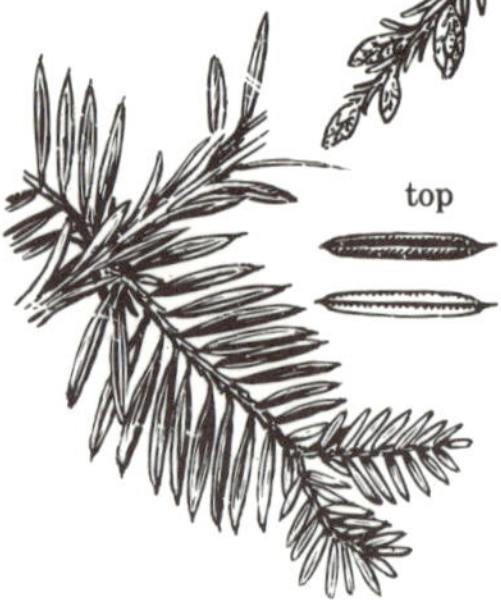

Leaves Flattened, sharply pointed needles, 1.5-2 cm long, growing in two rows on either side of the side shoots; dark green above and marked with two white bands beneath. The main shoots are covered with awl-shaped scale leaves, 6-8 mm long.

Description An evergreen conifer, to 40 m, with a columnar crown of horizontal or drooping branches and a distinctive straight tapering trunk. In its native California this tree grows much taller, reaching a height of more than 110m; it is considered to be the tallest-growing tree in the world.

Bark Thick, soft, fibrous and brownish-red, with deep cracks and holes in older trees.

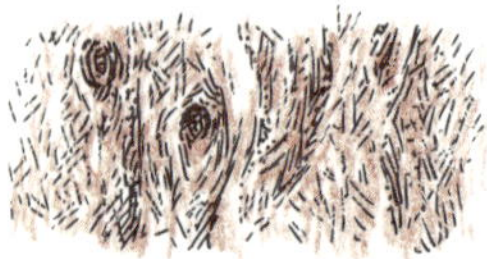

Habitat Mainly parks and gardens, where it is grown for ornament; occasionally planted for timber in plantations.
Range Introduced from W. North America; frequent in N.W. Europe.
Annual cycle: Male cones: February-April; female cones: February-October.

TAXODIACEAE

Leyland

Leyland cypress (*Cupressocyparis leylandii*). A similar and closely related tree, a widely grown hybrid. It can be distinguished from Lawson's cypress by its narrow, compact crown and its leaf sprays, which are less flattened.

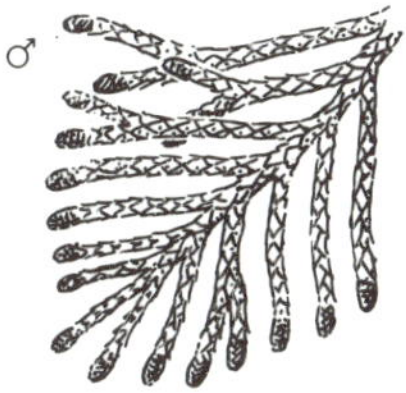

Male cones Club-shaped and crimson, 5 mm long, at the tips of the twigs, becoming yellow with pollen.

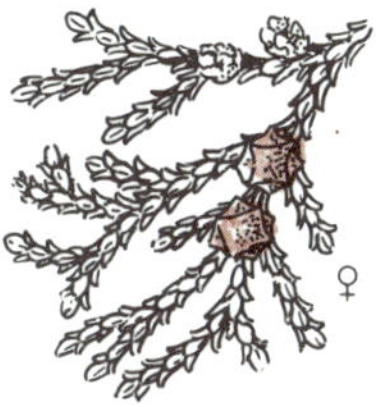

Female cones Bud-like and bluish, 5 mm long, ripening into small, round, pea-sized cones, at first green and finally brown, with lumpy scales.

Bark Smooth and dark brownish-green, becoming grey-brown and vertically cracked with age.

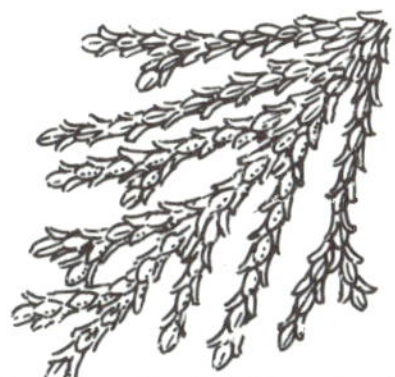

Leaves Scale-like, dark green above and paler beneath, and closely pressed to the twigs, which form flattened fern-like sprays. The leaves smell of parsley when crushed.

Description An evergreen conifer, to 38 m, with a dense pyramid-shaped crown the tip of which droops downwards. There are many cultivated varieties of this tree, of various shapes and with foliage ranging from golden-yellow to blue-grey; the original form is described below.

Habitat Parks, gardens, churchyards and large country estates, where it is grown for ornament; occasionally seen in plantations.

Range Introduced from W. North America; common and widespread in all parts of Europe.

Annual cycle Male cones: March-April; female cones: March-November.

Juniper *Juniperus communis*

CUPRESSACEAE

Leaves Sharp-pointed needles, to 1 cm growing in whorls of three on the twigs. They are blue-green marked with a white band on the upper surface, grey-green beneath.

Male cones Small, yellow and cylindrical, borne in clusters on the twigs.

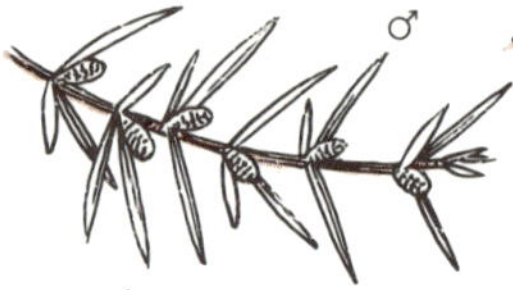

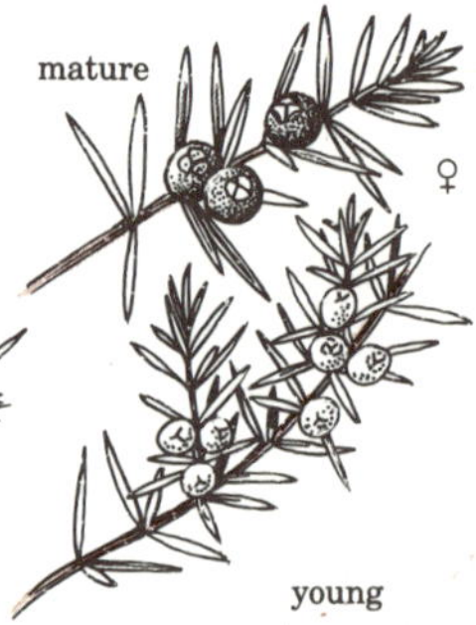

Female cones Small, bud-like and green, ripening into berry-like cones, 6-9 mm long, at first green and finally blue. The ripe berries are used for flavouring gin and have a characteristic smell of gin when crushed.

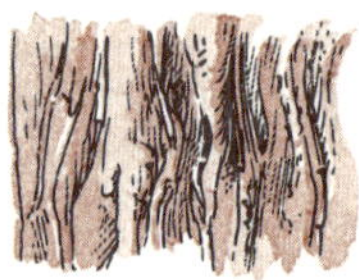

Bark Thin, flaking and bluish-grey.

Description An evergreen conifer, to 6 m, either with a narrow pointed crown or growing as a low broad shrub with spreading branches. There are separate male and female trees.

Habitat Grows naturally in a variety of habitats, typically chalkland, limestone areas, moors and heaths.
Range N. Europe to S.W. Asia; widespread and common.
Annual cycle Male cones: March-April; female cones: March-October (take 2 years to ripen).

TAXACEAE

Leaves Flattened, pointed needles, 2-4 cm long, arranged in two rows on the shoots, very dark green above and paler green beneath. The leaves are poisonous.

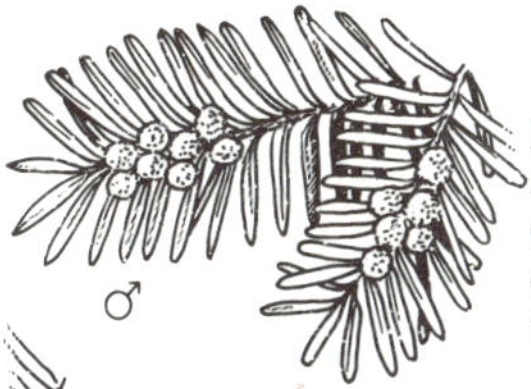

Male cones Rounded and yellowish, about 6 mm long, growing in clusters on the undersides of the shoots.

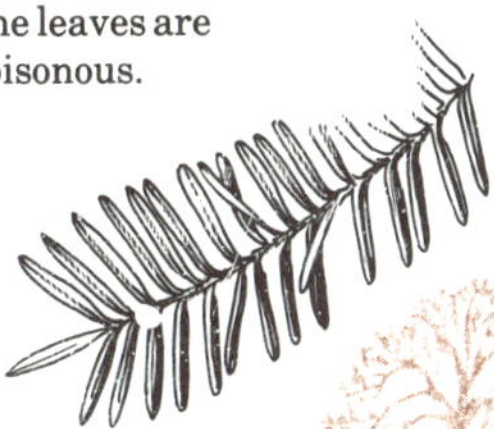

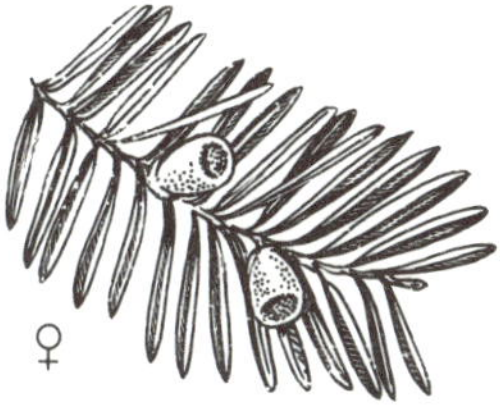

Female cones Tiny, bud-like and green, borne singly on the shoots and ripening into fleshy cup-like red structures about 1 cm long, each enclosing a single seed. The seeds (but not the fleshy part) are poisonous.

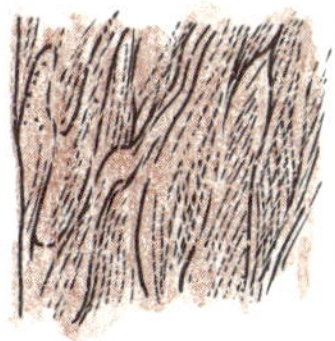

Description An evergreen conifer, to 25 m (most trees are 10-15 m), with a dense broad crown and very dark foliage. There are usually separate male and female trees. The Irish yew is a commonly cultivated variety with upright branches.

Bark Thin and reddish- or purplish-brown, flaking away in thin vertical strips to leave bare red patches.

Habitat Grows wild on chalkland and limestone areas and in oakwoods; widely planted for ornament in churchyards, parks and gardens.
Range Europe to S.W. Asia; common and widespread.
Annual cycle Male cones: February-April; female cones: February-November.

Monkey puzzle *Araucaria araucana*

ARAUCARIACEAE

Female cones Rounded and green, to about 7.5 cm, growing singly and upright at the branch tips. Ripen to large, round, spiny brown cones, to 15 cm, the scales of which are shed to release large bright brown edible seeds.

Male cones Cylindrical, to 10 cm, borne in groups of 2 or 3 at the tips of the topmost branches. At first green, they become yellow with pollen and finally brown.

Leaves Dark green, leathery and triangular with sharp points, 10mm long and 6 mm broad, arranged in overlapping whorls all round the shoots.

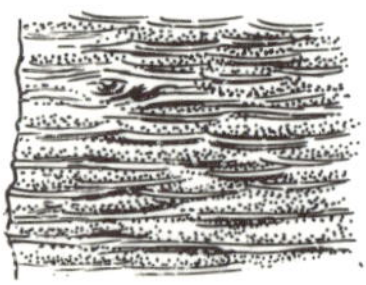

Bark Dark grey and horizontally wrinkled, marked with scars of old branches that have fallen off.

Description An evergreen conifer, to 30 m, with a straight trunk and a very distinctive rounded crown of symmetrically arranged branches with upturned ends. There are usually separate male and female trees. Also known as the Chile pine.

Habitat Parks and gardens, where it is grown for ornament.
Range Introduced from Chile and Argentina; common and widespread in Europe.
Annual cycle Male cones: June-July; female cones: June-October (take 2 years to ripen).

SALICACEAE

White poplar (*P. alba*). It is taller than the aspen (to 30 m), its whitish bark has diamond-shaped markings, and the leaves on the upper part of the tree are three- to five-lobed, dark green above and white beneath. Common and widely distributed.

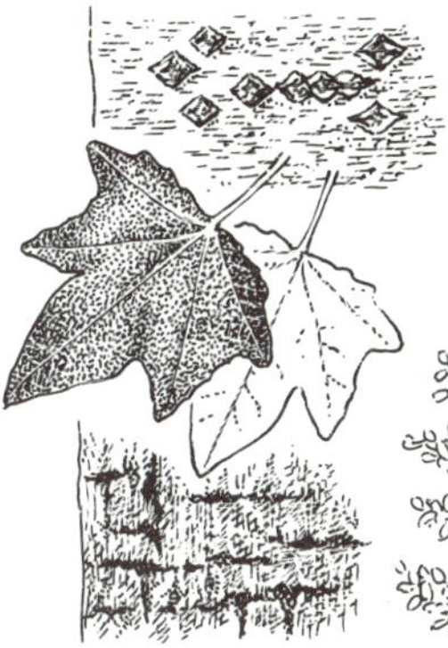

Leaves Almost round with wavy edges, 4-6 cm long and 5-7 cm broad, coppery-brown at first, becoming greyish-green above and paler beneath, and finally rich yellow in autumn. They have flat stalks, 4-6 cm long. Leaves on the sucker shoots are triangular in shape.

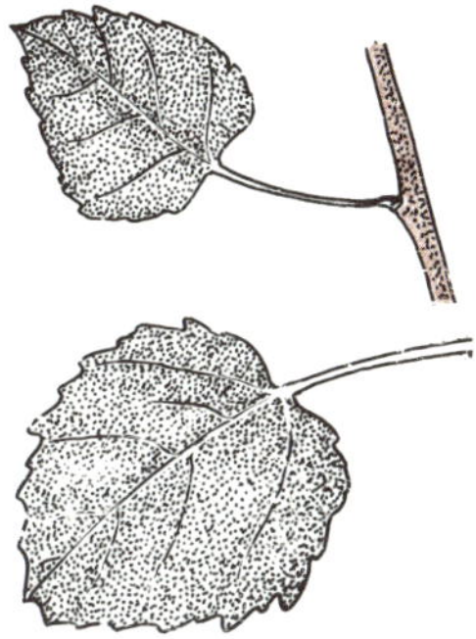

Bark Very smooth and greenish-grey, with darker horizontal wrinkles, becoming brownish and ridged at the base with age.

Male flowers Pinkish-brown catkins, 5-10 cm long, with silky grey hairs, becoming yellow with pollen and finally brown.

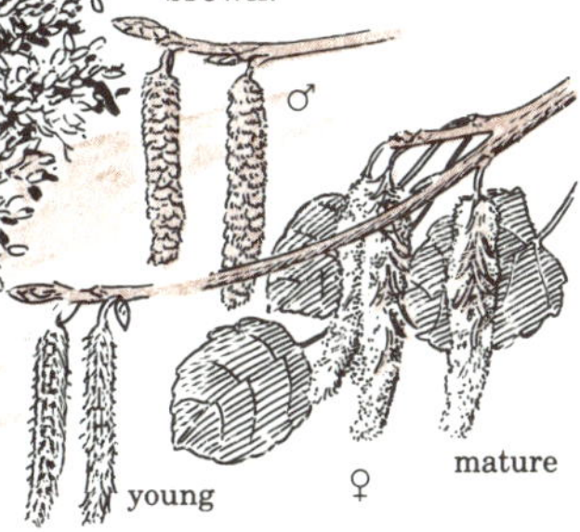

Description A deciduous tree, to 15 m, with a roughly conical and sparsely branched crown. It often produces suckers and the leaves tremble in the slightest breeze, which makes it easy to recognize at a distance. There are separate male and female trees.

Female flowers Green catkins, 10-12.5 cm long, with silky grey hairs, becoming fluffy and white with masses of seeds.

Habitat Grows wild in damp places on hillsides and river banks, in valleys, and at the edge of woods; its wood is used for matches.
Range Europe, Asia and N. Africa; widespread and common.
Annual cycle Male flowers: February-March; female flowers: February-June; leaves: May-November.

Lombardy poplar *Populus nigra italica*

SALICACEAE

Description A graceful deciduous tree, to 30 m or more, easily recognized by its tall, narrow, spire-like crown of upswept branches. The branches often start very low down on the trunk. The tree is a cultivated variety of the black poplar (*P. nigra*), and there are separate male and female trees (most trees are male).

Winter buds Slender, pointed and reddish-brown, to 8 mm.

Leaves Bright-green and triangular, 6cm long and 4.5 cm broad, with toothed margins.

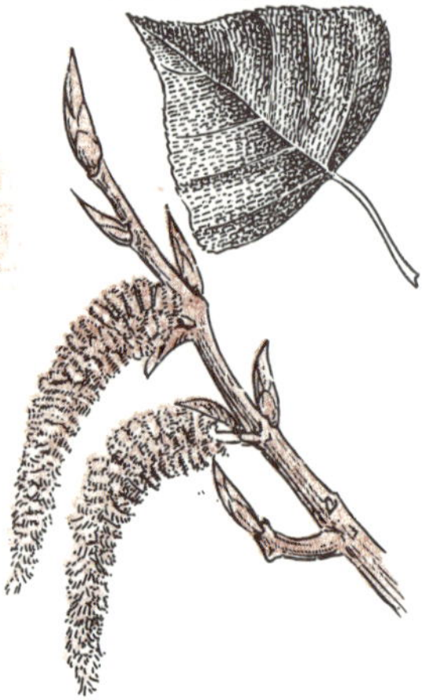

Bark Grey and smooth at first, becoming darker, ridged and bearing small twiggy branches with age.

Male flowers Deep-red catkins, to 5 cm, becoming yellow as they shed pollen. They appear before the leaves.

Habitat Roadsides, parks and gardens, where it is planted for ornament or shelter.
Range Europe; widespread and very common.
Annual cycle Male flowers: March-April; leaves: May-October.

SALICACEAE

Weeping willow (*S.* × *chrysocoma*). Another common willow, widely planted for ornament in gardens and parks and by rivers. Like the crack willow it has narrow pointed leaves but is easily distinguished by its long flexible yellow twigs, which hang down to the ground.

Winter buds Yellowish-brown, slender and pointed, closely pressed to the twigs.

Female flowers Green catkins, to 10 cm, eventually releasing fluffy white seeds.

♀

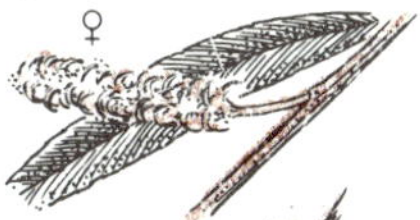

Male flowers Yellow catkins, 2-5 cm long.

♂

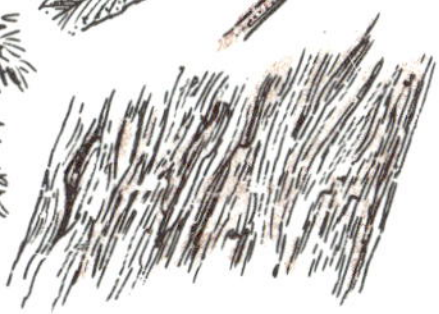

Bark Dark grey and scaly, becoming thickly ridged with age.

Leaves Long, narrow and pointed, to 12 cm, with toothed margins. They are a rich glossy green above and pale grey-green beneath.

Description A deciduous tree, to 25 m, with a spreading rounded crown of upturned branches. It takes its name from the fact that twigs snap off readily from their bases when pulled away. There are separate male and female trees.

Habitat Grows wild on river and stream banks and in marshes and damp woods.
Range Europe, W. and S.W. Asia; common and widespread.
Annual cycle Leaves: April-October; male flowers: April-May; female flowers: April-June.

Goat willow *Salix capraea*

SALICACEAE

Leaves Oval and pointed-tipped with wavy margins, to 10 cm long and 6 cm broad, dark grey-green above and paler and hairy beneath. Their stalks are dark red and hairy.

Male flowers Egg-shaped catkins, to 3 cm, silvery-grey and silky at first, becoming yellow with pollen. They appear long before the leaves.

Winter buds Pointed, oval and bright red, 3-4 mm long.

Female flowers Egg-shaped catkins, 5-6 cm long, whitish and silky at first, becoming green and finally white and fluffy with seeds. They appear long before the leaves.

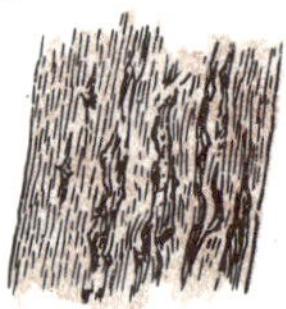

Bark Smooth and grey when young, becoming brown with wide shallow cracks with age.

Description A deciduous small tree or shrub, to about 10 m, with a spreading crown of upturned branches. It can be easily recognized in late winter when its catkins appear on the bare branches. There are separate male and female trees. Also known as the pussy willow or sallow.

Habitat Grows wild in damp woods, scrub and hedges, often near water.
Range Europe to N.E. Asia; common and widespread.
Annual cycle Male flowers: February-April; female flowers: February-May; leaves: late April-October.

JUGLANDACEAE

Female flowers Green and flask-shaped, growing in groups of 2 to 5 at the tips of the shoots.

Fruit Green and rounded, enclosing the familiar edible nut in its pale brown shell. Unripe fruits are gathered to make pickled walnuts.

Male flowers Greenish-yellow catkins, 5-10 cm long.

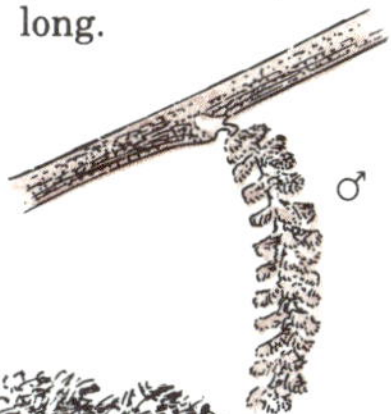

Winter buds Small, broad, rounded and purplish-brown.

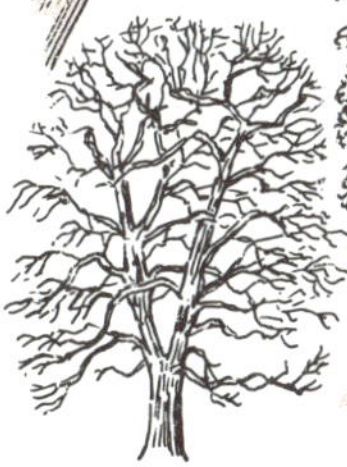

Leaves Compound, with 7 to 9 leaflets arranged in pairs on the stem and a single one at the tip. Each leaflet is oval, pointed and leathery, 6-18 cm long, at first orange-brown and later dull green. When crushed they have a strong aromatic smell and stain the fingers brown.

Description A large deciduous tree, to 30 m, with a broad rounded crown of widely spreading twisting branches. In winter the tree can be recognized by these branches and by its distinctive bark.

Bark Pale grey and smooth, with wide cracks.

Habitat Parks and gardens, where it is grown for ornament.
Range Probably introduced from S.E. Europe and S.W. Asia; fairly common in N.W. Europe.
Annual cycle Leaves: May-October; male flowers: May-June; female flowers; May-June; fruit: July-October.

Common alder *Alnus glutinosa*

BETULACEAE

Female flowers Club-shaped and erect, 5-6 mm long, at first purple but becoming dark red and developing into a cone-like fruit.

Fruit Soft, green and egg-shaped, maturing into a dark brown woody cone, to 1.5 cm. Old cones that have shed their seeds may remain on the tree for a year or more.

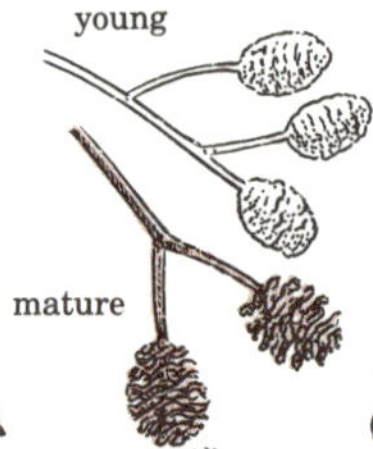

Male flowers Hanging catkins, 3-5 cm long, at first brown then becoming reddish-yellow with pollen.

Leaves Rounded, 10 cm long and 7 cm broad, with an indented tip and toothed margins. They are dark green above and paler beneath.

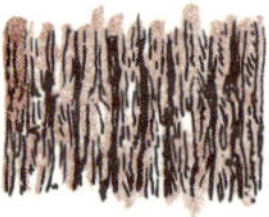

Bark Purplish-brown, becoming grey-brown and cracked into small square plates. In very old trees the bark is grey.

Winter buds Purplish-brown and club-shaped, to 7 mm, borne on a short stalk.

Description A deciduous tree, to 20 m or more, with a narrow conical crown when young, becoming broader, spreading and sparsely branched with age. In winter it can be easily recognized by its cones, which are present all the year round.

Habitat Grows wild on the banks of streams, lakes and rivers and in marshes.
Range Europe, W. Asia, and N. Africa; common and widespread.
Annual cycle Male flowers: February-March; female flowers: February-June; leaves: April-November; fruit: June-October.

Silver birch *Betula pendula*

BETULACEAE

Male flowers Pale purple-brown catkins, 2 cm long, becoming longer (to 3 cm), yellow with pollen and hanging down.

Female flowers and fruit Dark green erect catkins, to 1.5 cm, ripening into greenish-brown gherkin-shaped structures, 2-3 cm long, which hang down and break up on the tree to release the seeds.

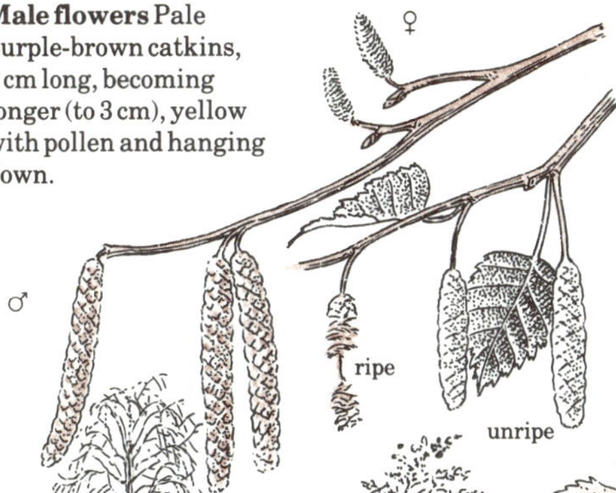

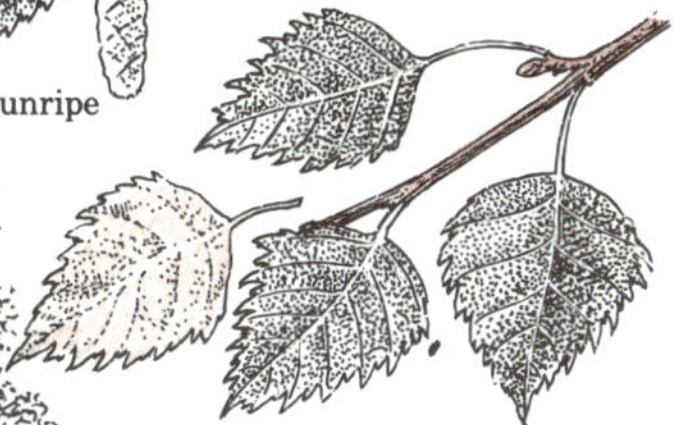

Leaves 3-7 cm long, with a wedge-shaped base, pointed tip and toothed margins. They are carried on slender stalks and turn from green to orange-yellow in autumn.

Winter buds Green and conical, to 4 mm, becoming sticky with resin. The twigs bearing them have raised white warty patches.

Bark Silvery-white and thin, with darker horizontal lines, peeling off to reveal black diamond-shaped patches. At the base of the trunk of old trees are black ridges and knobbly plates.

Description A graceful deciduous tree, to 30 m, with a high-domed crown and long slender twigs hanging down from the tips of the branches. It can be recognized in winter by its shape and its distinctive bark.

Habitat Grows wild on hills and moors and in woods and scrub; also cultivated for ornament.
Range Europe and S.W. Asia; common and widespread.
Annual cycle Male flowers: November-April; female flowers and fruit: March-November; leaves: April-October.

Hornbeam *Carpinus betulus*

BETULACEAE

Leaves Oval and pointed, to 10 cm long and 6.5 cm broad, with sharply toothed margins and prominent parallel veins. They are dark green above, yellowish-green beneath, and turn golden-yellow in autumn.

Male flowers Hanging catkins, 2.5-5 cm long, becoming reddish-yellow as they shed pollen.

Female flowers Hanging green leafy catkins, to 3 cm long.

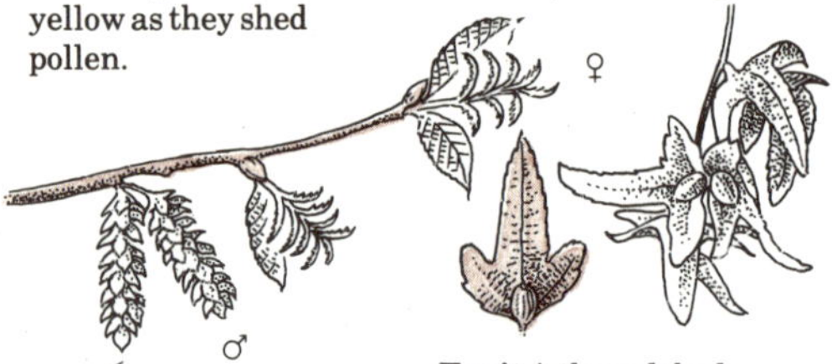

Fruit A three-lobed leafy bract, 3.5 cm long, bearing a pair of ridged nutlets at the base. They grow in clusters of 6 to 8.

Bark Smooth and grey, with a network of silvery and brown veins. The trunk itself is folded into deep rounded ridges (flutes).

Description A deciduous tree, to 25 m or more, with a domed crown of ascending branches. It has a distinctive trunk with rounded vertical ridges (flutes), by which it can be recognized in winter. Hornbeam is often used for hedges as it retains golden-yellow dead leaves throughout the winter if clipped down to hedge size.

Winter buds Slender, pointed and pale brown, 6-7 mm long, closely pressed to the twig.

Habitat Grows wild in woods and hedgerows; also cultivated as an ornamental hedge or tree.
Range Europe and S.W. Asia; common and widespread.
Annual cycle Male flowers: March-April; female flowers: March-July; leaves: April-October; fruit: August-November.

CORYLACEAE

Fruit Hard, smooth, rounded edible nuts, 1.5-2cm long, each enclosed in a leafy bract. They ripen from green to pink-brown.

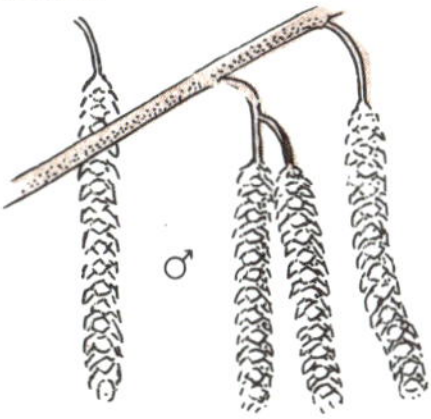

Male flowers Brownish-yellow catkins, becoming yellow as they shed pollen and growing to 5 cm long.

Female flowers Small brown bud-like structures, 3-5 mm long, with a tuft of red stigmas at the tip.

Bark Smooth and grey-brown, with small raised patches.

Leaves Rounded, to 10 cm long and broad, with a pointed tip and sharply toothed margins. They are deep green and hairy above, paler and downy beneath, turning yellow in autumn.

Winter buds Smooth, oval and blunt-tipped.

Description A deciduous bush or small tree, to 12 m, with a broad rounded crown. It is easily recognized in late winter, when male catkins are conspicuous on bare branches.

Habitat Grows wild in woods and hedgerows; also cultivated as hedging and for its nuts.
Range Europe and S.W. Asia; very common and widespread.
Annual cycle Male flowers: December-March; female flowers: March-April; leaves: May-November; fruit: August-October.

Beech *Fagus sylvatica*

FAGACEAE

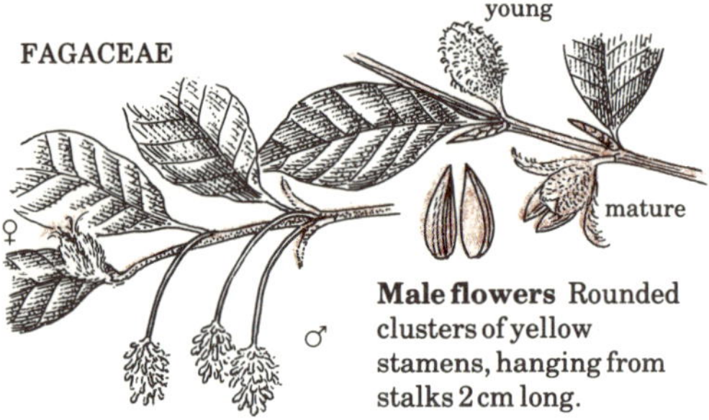

Fruit A prickly husk, 2.5 cm long, ripening from green to brown and splitting to release two shiny brown triangular nuts (beech mast).

Male flowers Rounded clusters of yellow stamens, hanging from stalks 2 cm long.

Leaves Oval and pointed, to 10 cm long and 7 cm broad, with strongly marked parallel veins and slightly wavy margins. They are a shiny dark green above, paler beneath, turning yellow and finally orange-brown in autumn.

Female flowers Rounded tufts of thread-like stigmas surrounded by reddish thread-like bracts; borne on short hairy stalks.

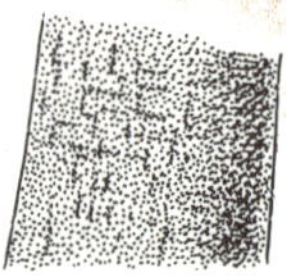

Bark Smooth and silvery-grey, often with a network of fine ridges.

Description A large deciduous tree, to 30 m, with a domed crown of spreading branches. It has a distinctive smooth grey trunk and long winter buds, by which it can be recognized in winter. Young trees and beech hedges retain their dead bronze-coloured leaves all winter. There are various cultivated forms, notably the copper beech with purple leaves.

Winter buds Slender, long and pointed, to 2 cm, with many scales.

Habitat Grows wild forming large woods on chalk and limestone; also widely cultivated in parks and gardens.
Range Much of Europe; common and widespread.
Annual cycle Leaves: May-early November; male flowers: May; female flowers: May-June; fruit: August-October.

FAGACEAE

Flowers Long, conspicuous, feathery yellow catkins, to 32 cm. The longest catkins carry only male flowers; shorter ones have greenish female flowers at their bases and unopened male flowers at the tips.

Leaves Large, oblong and pointed-tipped, to 20 cm long and 10 cm broad, with prominent parallel veins and strongly toothed margins. Glossy dark green above and paler beneath, they turn yellow and finally brown in autumn.

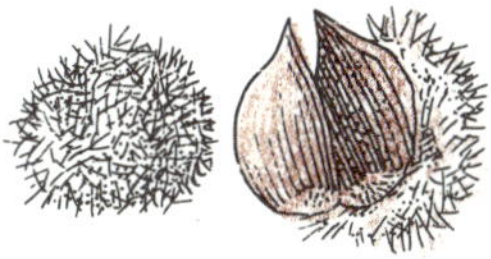

Fruit A pale green spiny husk, 3 cm long and 4 cm broad, splitting when ripe to release 1 or 2 shiny brown edible nuts.

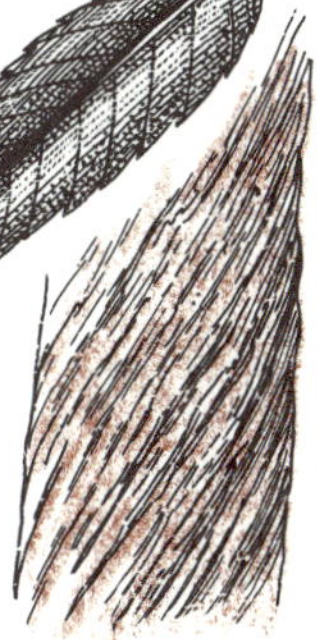

Bark Grey-brown to dark brown, with deep narrow vertical ridges that form a spiral in mature trees.

Description A deciduous tree, to 30 m, with a tall narrow-domed crown of twisting branches. Mature trees can be recognized in winter by their shape and characteristic stout spirally ridged trunk.

Winter buds Small, oval and reddish-brown.

Habitat Parks and gardens, where it is cultivated for ornament and nuts; also naturalized in some woods.
Range Introduced from S. Europe; fairly common and widespread.
Annual cycle Leaves: May-October; flowers: June-July; fruit: August-October.

English or pedunculate oak *Quercus robur*

FAGACEAE

Fruit An acorn, 1.5-4 cm long, carried in a shallow greenish knobbly cup on a stalk 4-8 cm long, ripening from whitish-green to dark brown.

Sessile or durmast oak (*Q. petraea*). It has a longer trunk, taller crown and straighter branches, its leaves have longer stalks and its acorns are stalkless.

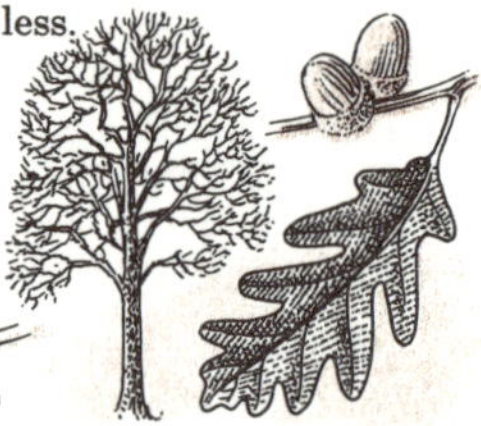

Leaves Oblong, 10-12 cm long, with smooth-edged lobes along the sides and two small lobes at the base. Borne on short stalks, they are a rich dull green above and paler beneath, turning yellow-orange in autumn. Often covered with small galls.

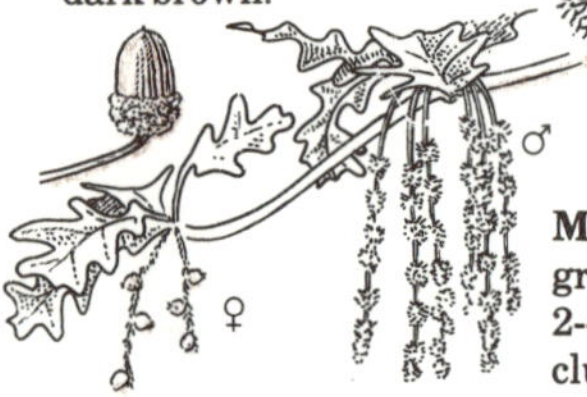

Male flowers Slender greenish-yellow catkins, 2-4 cm long, growing in clusters on the twigs.

Female flowers Brownish-red globes, to 2 mm, growing on stalks at the tips of the twigs.

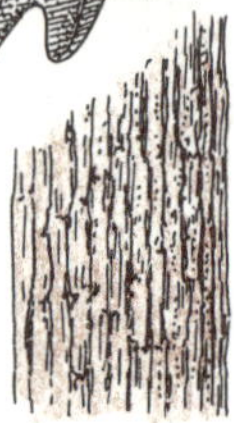

Bark Thick, grey and rugged, deeply cracked into small irregular patches.

Winter buds Short, stout, pointed and pale brown, with many overlapping scales, occurring singly along the twigs and in clusters at the tips.

Description A rugged deciduous tree, to 30 m or more, with a short stout trunk supporting a broad crown of spreading twisting branches. In winter the tree can be recognized by its distinctive shape, rugged bark and the clusters of buds at the twig tips.

Habitat Forms natural woods in lowland areas, especially on clay soils; widely planted for timber and ornament in parks, gardens and forests.
Range Europe to S.W. Asia; widespread and common.
Annual cycle Leaves: late April-October; flowers: late April-May; fruit: August-October.

FAGACEAE

Leaves Variable in shape, but typically oval and pointed at each end, 5-10 cm long and 3-8 cm broad, with a smooth outline. They are silvery-white when they open, becoming yellow and finally dark green and shiny above, pale fawn and hairy beneath. Young trees and low shoots bear spiny holly-like leaves.

Female flowers Small and inconspicuous, 2 mm long, with a grey-green globular base and pink stigmas, growing on stout hairy stalks.

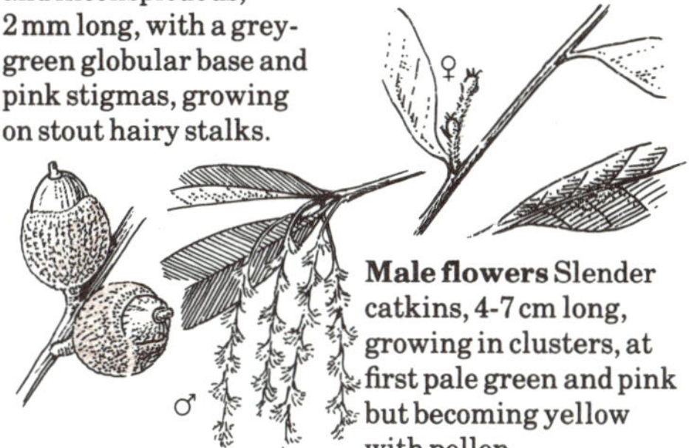

Male flowers Slender catkins, 4-7 cm long, growing in clusters, at first pale green and pink but becoming yellow with pollen.

Fruit A green acorn, 1.5-2 cm long, enclosed in a deep, scaly, greyish cup.

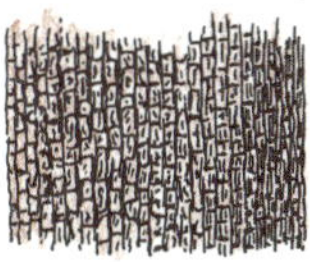

Bark Black or brownish-black, shallowly cracked into small, often curling squares.

Description An evergreen tree, to 28 m, with a very dense broad crown carried on a short stout trunk. The crown appears almost black in winter and silvery-grey in spring.

Habitat Parks and gardens, particularly in coastal areas, where it is grown for ornament and for shelter against sea winds.
Range Introduced from S. Europe; common in the rest of Europe.
Annual cycle Young leaves: from June; flowers; late May-June; fruit: August-October.

Wych elm *Ulmus glabra*

ULMACEAE

Smooth-leaved elm (*U. minor*). It differs from the wych elm chiefly in its narrower crown and its narrower leaves, which are shiny and leathery (not hairy) above. It is a native species.

↓

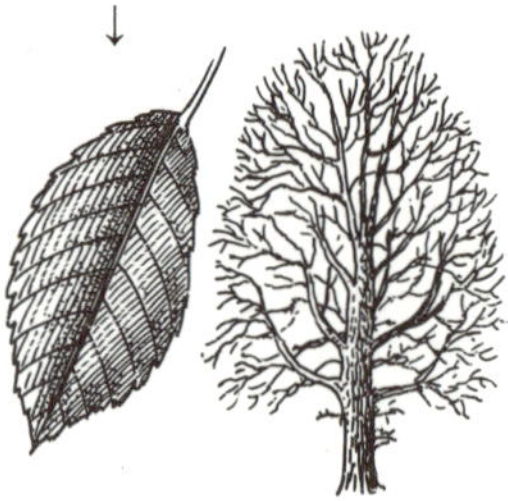

← **Flowers** Small and purplish-red, growing in dense rounded clusters on the shoots. They appear before the leaves and give the tree a reddish haze in early spring.

Fruit A flat rounded wing with a notched tip, 2.5 cm across, with a small nutlet at the centre. Growing in clusters, they are pale green and petal-like at first, becoming brown when ripe.

Bark Smooth and silvery-grey, becoming darker and cracked into a network of ridges with age.

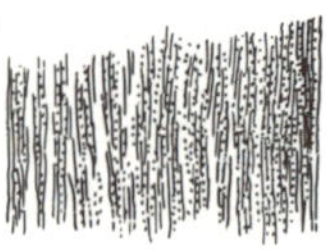

Leaves Oval, 10-18 cm long and 6-9 cm broad, with a pointed tip, toothed margins, prominent veins and a lopsided base, borne on a very short thick stalk. They are dark green above, paler beneath, and feel very rough, being covered with short bristly hairs.

Description A tall deciduous tree, to 38 m, with a broad rounded crown and a fan-shaped arrangement of stout branches arising from a short trunk.

Habitat Grows wild in woods and hedgerows, especially near water; also cultivated in parks and squares for ornament.
Range N. and C. Europe and W. Asia; common in N.W. Europe.
Annual cycle Flowers: February-March; fruit: March-July; leaves: April-November.

Flowers Large and goblet-shaped, with petals to 10 cm long that are white tinged with pink on the outside and white within. They appear before the leaves. Flowers of cultivated varieties range from white to pink.

Fruit A long pointed cone-like structure, made up of ripened carpels that split to release red seeds.

MAGNOLIACEAE

Leaves Oblong, 13 cm long and 5 cm broad, tapering at both ends, and glossy green, turning yellow in autumn.

Winter buds Green, oval and pointed, covered with down and pinched in at the base.

Description A deciduous ornamental shrub or small tree, to 7.5 m, with a broad rounded crown of spreading branches on a short, often divided, trunk. The tree is unmistakable in early spring, when its beautiful pale pink flowers open on bare branches.

Habitat Parks and gardens, where it is grown for ornament.
Range Europe; widespread and common.
Annual cycle Flowers: April-July; leaves: May-October; fruit: August-November.

54 **London plane** *Platanus × hispanica;*

PLATANACEAE

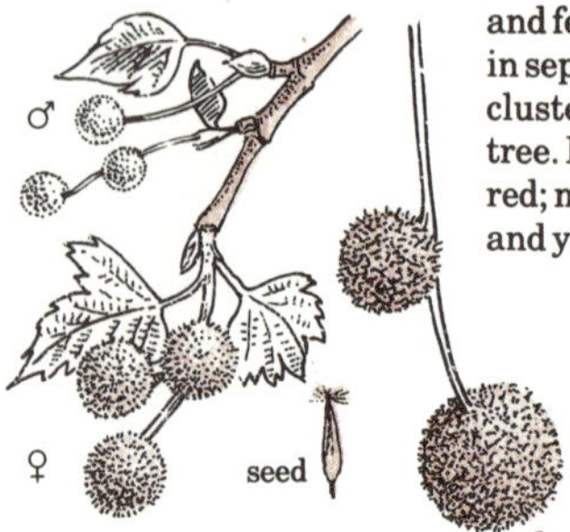

Flowers Small male and female flowers grow in separate rounded clusters on the same tree. Female clusters are red; males are smaller and yellowish.

Leaves Glossy and bright green above, paler beneath, to 20 cm long and 23 cm broad, divided into five pointed toothed lobes. They turn yellow or orange in autumn.

Fruit Brown, globular and hairy, to 8 cm, breaking up to release small conical hairy seeds.

Bark Thin and greyish-brown or greyish-green, flaking off to leave conspicuous yellow patches.

Winter buds Reddish-brown, 6-8 mm long, with a single scale, curved tip and protruding base.

Description A fast-growing deciduous tree, to 35 m, with a domed crown and wide-spreading branches supported on a long straight trunk. In winter it can be recognized by its bark and fruits.

Habitat Streets, squares, parks and gardens, where it is grown for ornament and shade.
Range W. and C. Europe; quite widespread and common.
Annual cycle Leaves: May-November; flowers: May; fruits: September-April.

ROSACEAE

Fruit Dark-red oval berries (haws), 8-10 mm long, each having a withered style at its tip and containing one seed.

Leaves Small (about 3.5 cm long and 4 cm broad) and shiny dark green with 3 to 7 lobes, which are often toothed.

Flowers Small and cup-shaped, each with five white petals and numerous pink stamens. They are borne in dense clusters.

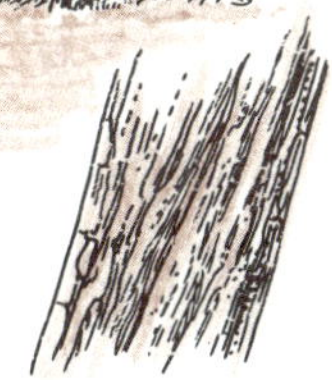

Twigs and winter buds The twigs bear short spines, set singly, and very small reddish-black scaly winter buds.

Bark Smooth and greyish-brown in young trees, flaking into small thin plates and becoming darker, rugged and fluted with age.

Description A deciduous thorny bush or tree, to 14 m, with a rounded densely branched crown. It can be easily recognized when it flowers in spring and bears berries in autumn; in winter its thorny branches are characteristic.

Habitat Grows wild in hedgerows, scrub, the edges of woods and hill-sides; also planted for ornament and hedging.
Range Europe; widespread and very common.
Annual cycle Leaves: May-October; flowers: May-June; fruit: August-October.

56 Crab apple *Malus sylvestris*

ROSACEAE

Leaves Oval or rounded, 5-6 cm long and 3-4 cm broad, with a pointed tip and toothed margins, borne on a 2.5 cm long reddish stalk. They are smooth and green above, paler and downy beneath.

Flowers To 3.5 cm across, each with five white or pink-tinged petals and many yellow stamens.

Fruit A small apple indented at each end, 2.5 cm across, green marked with white spots, ripening to yellow. They are too sour to be eaten raw but are made into jellies and jams.

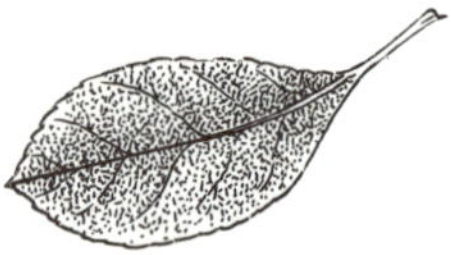

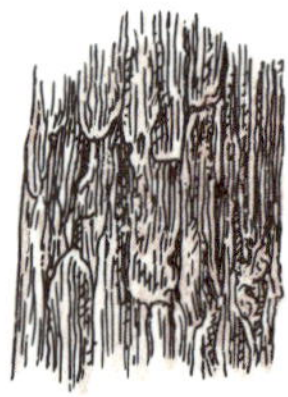

Bark Smooth and grey-brown, becoming wrinkled and scaly and flaking into small plates.

Winter buds Small and pointed, to 5 mm, purple-brown and fringed with grey hairs.

Description A small, spiny deciduous tree, to 10 m, with a dense broad crown of twisting branches carried on a short trunk. It is one of the ancestors of the cultivated orchard apple. In late spring its white or pale pink blossom is distinctive.

Habitat Grows wild in woods, hedgerows, and thickets.
Range Europe to S.W. Asia; quite common and widespread.
Annual cycle Leaves: May-October: flowers: May-June; fruit: July-October.

ROSACEAE

Fruit A cherry, 2.5 cm across, growing in clusters on long (to 5 cm) stalks and ripening from yellow to blackish-red.

Winter buds Oval, pointed and shiny red-brown, with many scales.

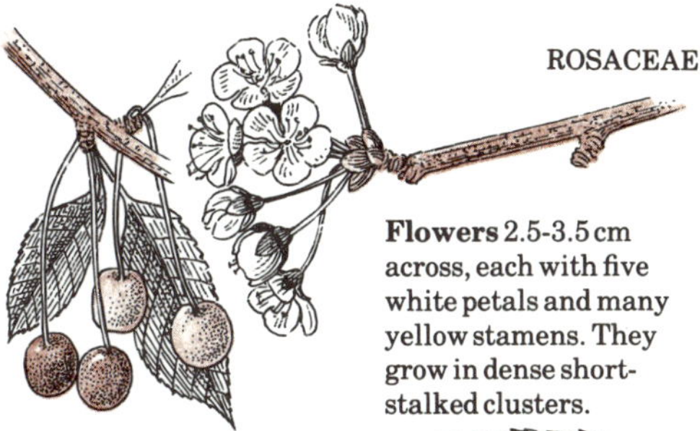

Flowers 2.5-3.5 cm across, each with five white petals and many yellow stamens. They grow in dense short-stalked clusters.

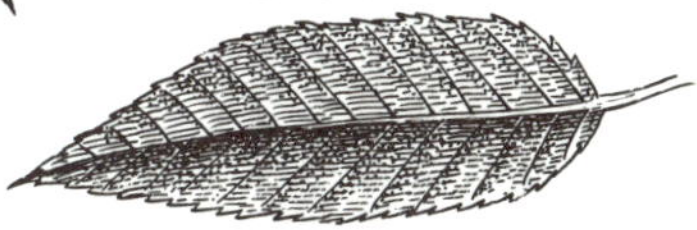

Leaves Oval and sharply pointed, to 10 cm long and 7 cm broad, the margins indented by forward-pointing teeth. They turn from green to orange and finally red before falling. The leafstalk, to 3.5 cm long, is red above and yellow beneath, with two lumpy glands near the base of the leaf.

Bark Reddish-brown with a metallic lustre, marked with prominent horizontal bands of breathing pores, becoming darker, scaly, and peeling off in old trees.

Description A tall, slender deciduous tree, to 20 m or more, with a straight trunk supporting an open rounded crown of up-spreading branches. It is an ancestor of orchard varieties. Its white flowers open in spring just before the leaves and in winter its bark is a distinctive feature.

Habitat Grows wild in woods, thickets, hedgerows, etc.; also planted for ornament in parks and gardens.
Range Europe, N. Africa, and W. Asia; common and widespread.
Annual cycle Flowers: April-May; leaves: April-October; fruit: June-July.

Almond *Prunus dulcis*

ROSACEAE

Fruit A leathery flattened oval structure, to 4 cm, covered with hairs and ripening from yellowish-green to dark brown. It splits to reveal the familiar nut – a woody pale-brown stone containing the edible kernel.

Japanese 'Kanzan' flowering cherry (*P.* '*Kanzan*'). Another very popular flowering ornamental tree. Its profuse deep pink double flowers open in May, along with the leaves.

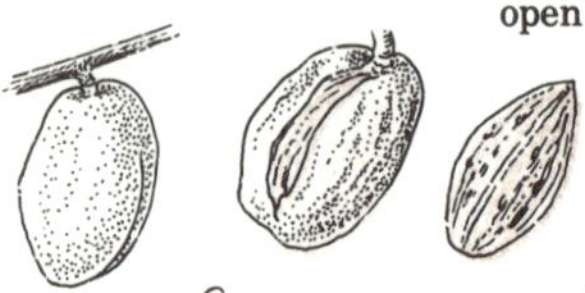

Leaves 7-12 cm long, narrow, pointed, and finely toothed. They are often folded into a V along the midrib.

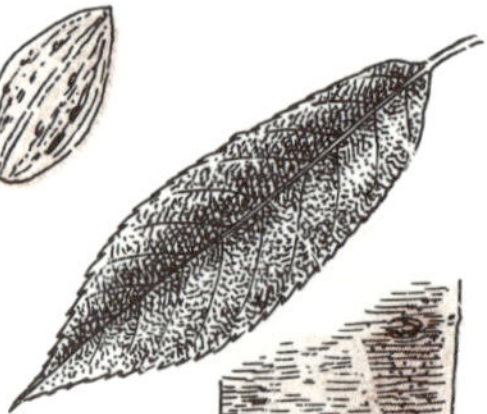

Flowers 3-5 cm across, each with five pale-pink petals and many pink-tipped stamens and borne on a short stalk. They open well ahead of the leaves. Many cultivated forms have double flowers.

Bark Smooth and dark purple-grey to blue-black, scattered with grey horizontal breathing pores, cracked into small square plates in old trees.

Description A small deciduous ornamental tree, to 9 m, with an open rounded crown of ascending branches. The tree is easily recognized in early spring, when its pink flowers open on bare branches.

Habitat Parks, gardens, streets, where it is planted for ornament.
Range Probably native to W. Asia and N. Africa but long and widely cultivated in N.W. Europe for its ornamental flowers.
Annual cycle Flowers: late February-April; leaves: April-October; fruit: August-December.

ROSACEAE

Fruit Rounded, 1.2 cm across, with acid-tasting flesh enclosing a hard stone. It ripens from green to blue-black and is covered with a white waxy bloom. Sloes are used for making jam and flavouring gin.

Leaves Small (2-4 cm long), oval, and dull green, with a pointed tip and finely toothed margins. They are borne on short reddish stalks.

Flowers Star-shaped, about 1.2 cm across, with five white petals and longish orange-tipped stamens. They usually appear before the leaves.

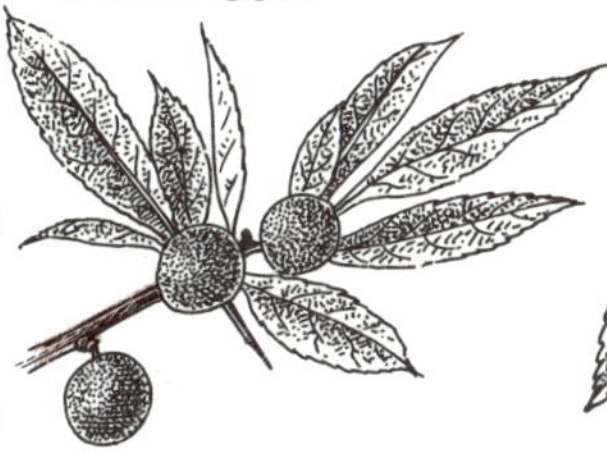

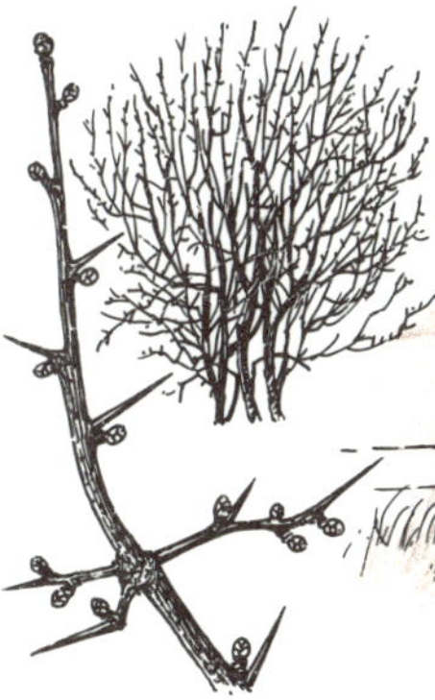

Bark Smooth and purplish-black.

Twigs and winter buds The twigs bear sharp spines and very small oval purplish-black winter buds.

Description A deciduous spiny shrub or small tree, to 6 m, with a dense, rather shapeless crown on a short and often forked trunk. It tends to form thickets and is unmistakable in early spring, when its white flowers open on bare spiny branches.

Habitat Grows wild on banks, hillsides, the edges of woods and in hedgerows and scrub.
Range Europe and N. Asia; common and widespread.
Annual cycle Flowers: March-April; leaves: April-October; fruit: August-October.

ROSACEAE

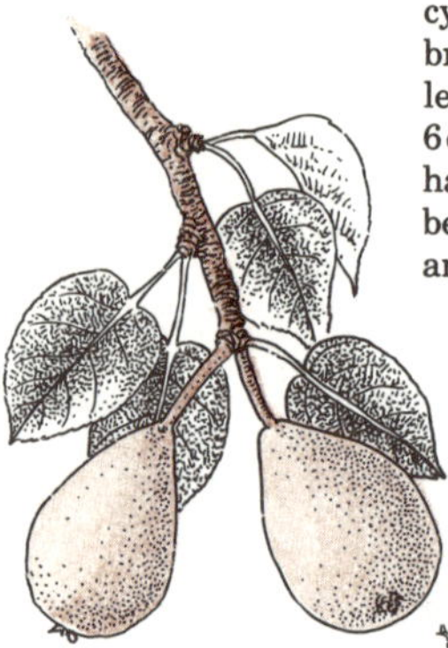

Fruit Narrow and cylindrical, becoming broader at the tip and lengthening to about 6 cm. Green at first, with hard woody flesh, it becomes brown, softer, and sweet when ripe.

Leaves Oval, 5-8 cm long, with a pointed tip and finely toothed margins. Dark- or yellowish-green and glossy, they are borne on long (2-5 cm) stalks.

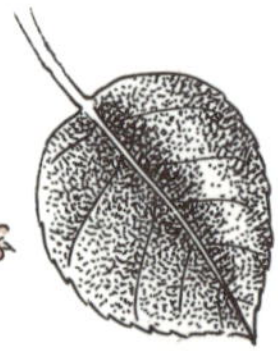

Bark Dark grey or brown, deeply cracked into small square plates.

Flowers To 3.5 cm across, each with five white petals and red-tipped stamens. They grow in clusters on short spur shoots and open just before or at the same time as the leaves.

Description A slender deciduous, sometimes spiny, tree, to 15 m, with a tall straight trunk supporting a conical or rounded crown of ascending branches. The ancestor of many orchard pear trees, it can be recognized by its shape and, in spring, by its white blossom.

Habitat Grows wild in hedgerows and at the edges of woods; cultivated varieties are common in orchards and gardens.
Range Europe and W. Asia; cultivated forms are common and widespread, wild trees are less common.
Annual cycle Leaves: April-November; flowers: May-June; fruit: July-October.

ROSACEAE

Leaves Compound, with 9 to 15 leaflets arranged in pairs on a reddish stalk with a single leaf at the tip. Each leaflet is narrow and pointed, to 6 cm long and 2 cm wide, with toothed margins (except near the base). Deep green above and paler beneath, they turn yellow or crimson in autumn.

Fruit A berry, 1 cm across, grouped in clusters and ripening from green to yellow and finally red.

Flowers Grow in dense flat-topped clusters, 10-15 cm across, on woolly stalks. Each flower is 1 cm across, with five creamy-white petals and many stamens.

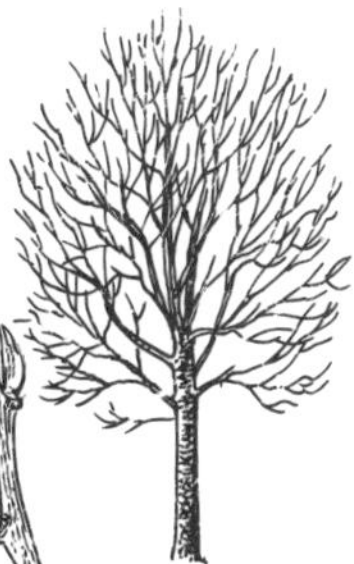

Bark Smooth and silvery-grey, marked with darker horizontal breathing pores; a network of thin scaly ridges develops in old trees.

Description A graceful deciduous tree, to 20 m, with a rounded or conical crown of slender upturned branches. It can be recognized easily at most times of the year, but especially in autumn, by its leaves and clusters of red berries.

Winter buds Long (1.7 cm), pointed and dark purple, with prominent hairy scales.

Habitat Grows wild on mountains (to 1000 m) and hillsides, woods and heaths; also planted for ornament in streets and gardens.
Range Europe, N. Africa, and S.W. Asia; widespread and common.
Annual cycle Leaves: April-November; flowers: May-June; fruit: August-October.

Whitebeam *Sorbus aria*

ROSACEAE

Flowers Grow in clusters 5-8 cm across on woolly stalks. Each flower, 1.5 cm across, has five white petals and many stamens.

Fruit A berry, 1.2 cm across, growing in clusters and ripening from green to red.

Leaves Oval, to 8 cm long and 5 cm broad, with a pointed tip and toothed margins. They are covered with dense silvery hairs when they first open; the upper surface becomes smooth and dark green and finally golden-brown in autumn, but the undersurface remains white and hairy.

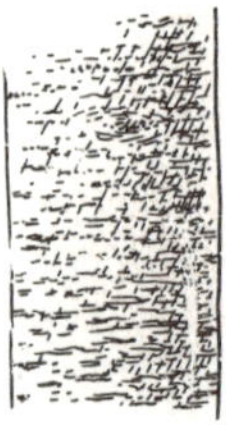

Bark Smooth and grey, developing thin scaly plates with age.

Description A deciduous tree, to 20 m, with a dense domed crown of upswept branches. The tree can be easily recognized at a distance by its leaves, which are white underneath and give the whole crown a silvery appearance, especially when they first open.

Winter buds Large (2 cm long), pointed, green, and sometimes hairy.

Habitat Grows wild on chalk and limestone, in woods, scrub, etc.; also planted for ornament in streets and gardens.
Range Europe; common both in the wild (in Britain and C. and S. Europe) and as an ornamental tree.
Annual cycle Leaves: April-November; flowers: May-June; fruit: July-October.

LEGUMINOSAE

Leaves Compound, composed of three pointed leaflets, each 2-6 cm long, dull-green above and grey-green with silky hairs beneath. The leaves have a stalk 2-6 cm long.

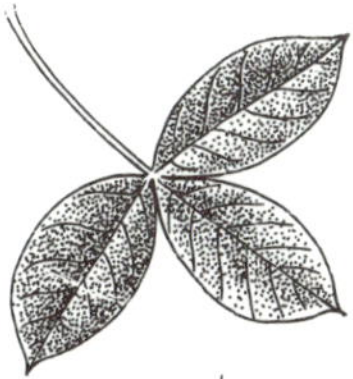

Fruit A slender dark brown leathery pod, 5-8 cm long, containing several black seeds. The pods hang in clusters, and both seeds and pods – like all parts of the plant – are very poisonous.

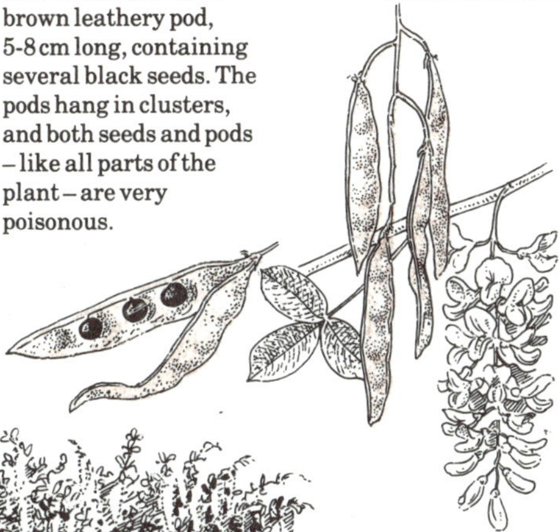

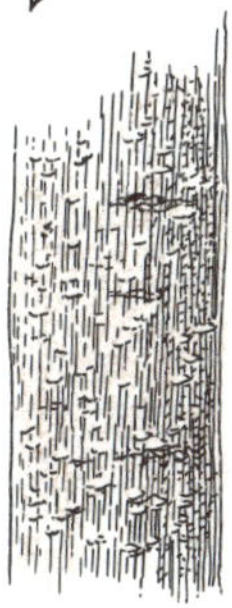

Flowers Bright yellow (often with reddish streaks), 2 cm long, and shaped like those of the sweet pea. They grow in conspicuous hanging clusters, 15-25 cm long.

Bark Smooth and greenish-brown, marked with darker patches of breathing pores.

Description A graceful deciduous ornamental tree, to 9 m, with an open irregular crown of ascending arching branches. Laburnum is unmistakable in early summer, with its hanging clusters of yellow flowers; the bark and leaves are also distinctive.

Winter buds Small, grey-brown and hairy, with pointed scales.

Habitat Parks, gardens, streets, etc., where it is grown for ornament.
Range Introduced from C. and S. Europe; common and widespread.
Annual cycle Leaves: May-October; flowers: May-June; fruit: August-October.

False acacia *Robinia pseudoacacia*

LEGUMINOSAE

Flowers Like those of laburnum but white and sweet-scented, hanging in dense clusters 10-20 cm long.

Fruit A slender dark-brown pod, 5-10 cm long, hanging in clusters on the tree throughout winter.

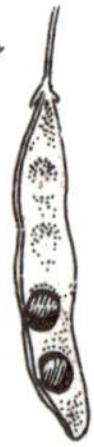

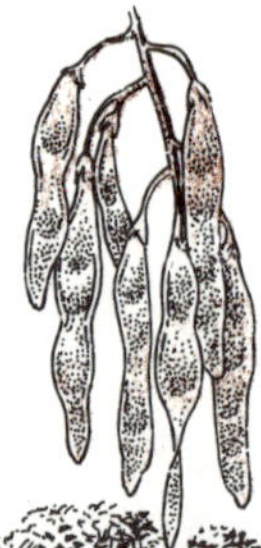

Leaves Compound, with 13 to 15 leaflets arranged in pairs on each side of the stalk and a single leaflet at the tip. Each leaflet is oval, 3.5 cm long and 2.5 cm broad, light green at first but becoming darker.

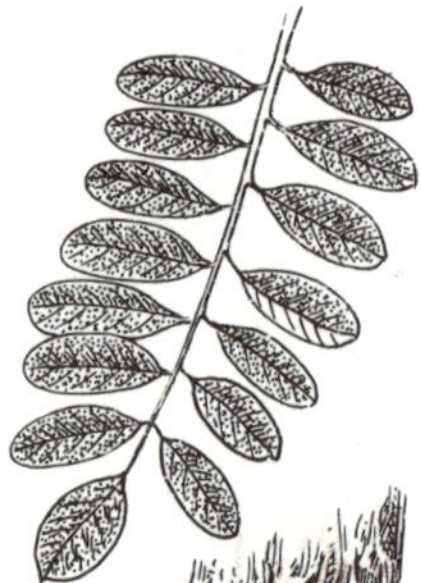

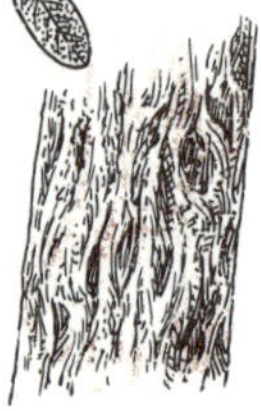

Bark Brown to dull grey and thick, with a network of deep ridges and hollows.

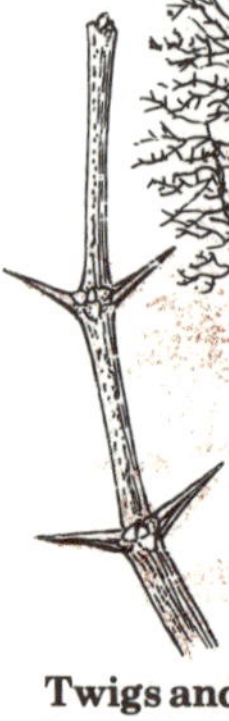

Twigs and winter buds Twigs bear a pair of short spines on the side of each bud; buds are very small.

Description A deciduous tree, to 25 m, with an irregular open crown of twisted branches supported on a short, often rugged, trunk. The light green foliage is distinctive and the tree can be recognized in winter by its shape and pods. Also known as robinia and locust tree.

Habitat Streets, parks, gardens, etc., where it is planted for ornament.
Range Introduced from E. North America; common in parts of N.W. Europe.
Annual cycle Leaves: May-November; flowers: June; fruit: September-February.

AQUIFOLIACEAE

Leaves Thick and leathery, 6-8 cm long, with a pointed tip and spiny margins. They are glossy dark green above, paler and matt beneath. Leaves at the top of the tree have smooth margins and some cultivated varieties have green and yellow leaves.

Flowers Both male and female flowers are small (6-8 mm) and sweet smelling, opening from round purple buds and each having four creamy-white petals and four stamens. They grow in dense clusters near the tips of the twigs.

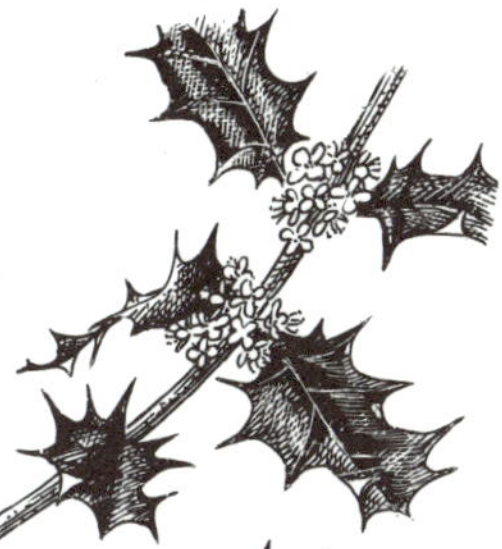

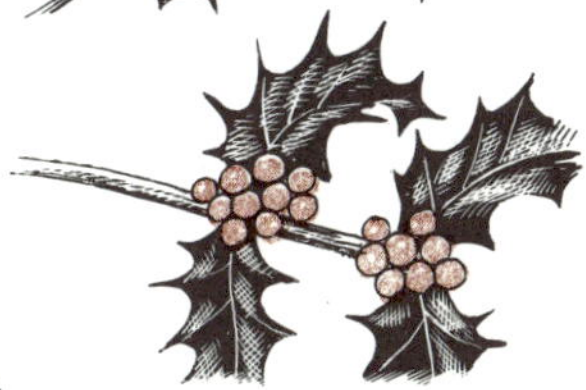

Fruit A round red berry, 7-10 mm across, enclosing four yellow seeds and growing in clusters.

Bark Smooth and grey, with darker markings and wartlike swellings in old trees.

Description An evergreen shrub or tree, to 20 m or more, in which the crown is narrow and conical when young, becoming broader, irregular and dense in old trees. Hollies are easily recognized by their spiny leaves and, in winter, red berries, familiar as Christmas decoration. There are separate male and female trees.

Habitat Grows wild in woods and hedges and on rocky hillsides; also planted in gardens, parks, etc., for ornament.
Range W, S, and C. Europe; widespread and common.
Annual cycle Flowers: May-June; fruit: October-February.

Spindle tree *Euonymus europaeus*

CELESTRACEAE

Leaves Narrow and oval, to 10 cm long, with a pointed tip and finely toothed margins. In autumn they turn from green to orange or crimson.

Flowers 1 cm across, with four greenish-white petals and four stamens. They grow in long-stalked clusters of 3 to 8.

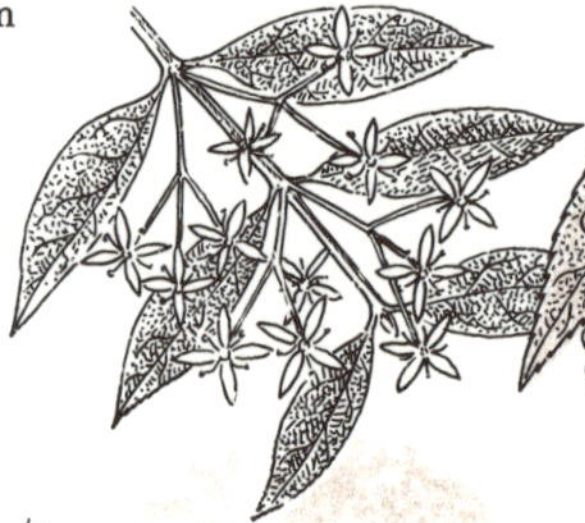

Fruit Red, fleshy and four-lobed, splitting when ripe to reveal four seeds each covered with a fleshy orange coat.

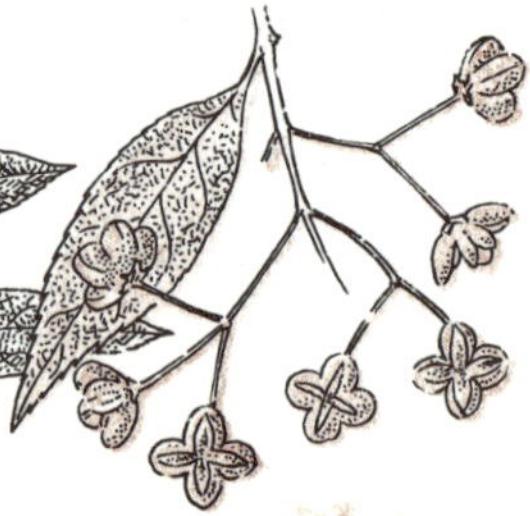

Winter buds Green and pointed, borne on green twigs.

Description A deciduous shrub or small tree, to 6 m, with a slender trunk supporting an open rounded crown of slender branches. In autumn its red fruits and crimson foliage are distinctive.

Bark Smooth and greenish, becoming grey or pale brown and crinkled in old trees.

Habitat Grows wild in woods, hedgerows and scrub, especially on limestone or chalky soils.
Range Europe (except the extreme north); common and widespread.
Annual cycle Leaves: May-October; flowers: May-June; fruit: September-October.

ACERACEAE

Leaves To 18 cm long and 25 cm wide, with up to five coarsely toothed pointed lobes. Borne on long (to 10 cm) red or yellow stalks, they open brownish and become dark green above, paler and hairy beneath.

Norway maple (*A. platanoides*). A similar and related tree, it is smaller than the sycamore (to 22 m), the flowers open before the leaves, and the two wings of the fruit are joined to form almost a straight line.

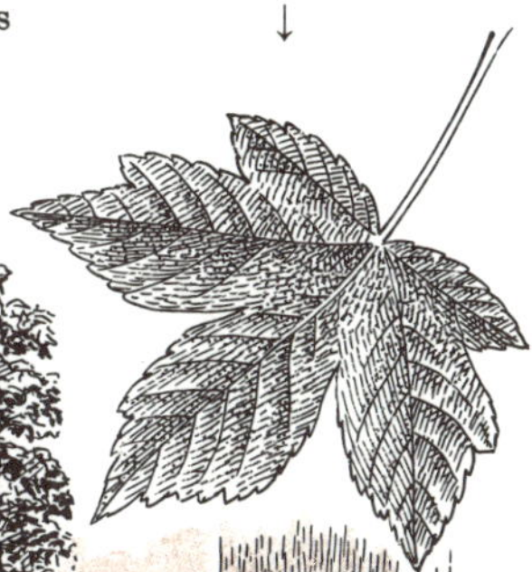

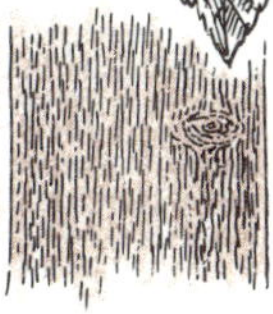

Fruit Two winged seeds, each 3 cm long, joined together at a right angle at their bases. They grow in clusters and ripen from green to red and finally brown.

Flowers Small and yellowish, growing in hanging clusters 6-12 cm long

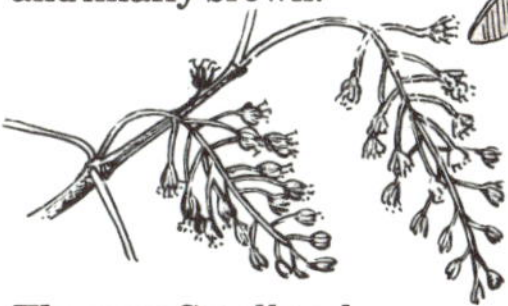

Bark Smooth and grey, becoming pinkish-brown and scaly with age.

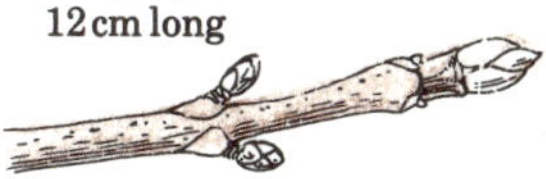

Winter buds Green, oval and pointed, growing in pairs on the twig.

Description A large deciduous tree, to 35 m, with a dense, domed, spreading crown of massive branches ending in twisted shoots. The winged fruits in late summer and autumn are a distinctive feature.

Habitat Gardens, parks, streets and squares, where it is planted for shade and ornament; also grows naturally in woods.
Range Introduced from S. and C. Europe; very common and widespread.
Annual cycle Leaves: April-October; flowers: April-May; fruit: July-October.

Horse chestnut *Aesculus hippocastaneum*

HIPPOCASTANACEAE

Flowers 2 cm across, with five fringed white petals tinged with pink or yellow at the base and long stamens. They are grouped in upright conical clusters, 15-30 cm long.

Fruit Green, globular and prickly, 6 cm across, splitting when ripe to release 1 to 3 shiny brown seeds (conkers), each with a pale circular patch.

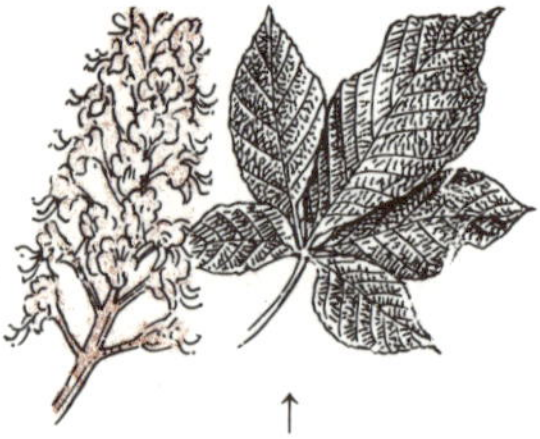

↑

Red horse chestnut (*A.* × *carnea*). It differs from the horse chestnut in its red flowers, smaller, darker crinkly leaves, less prickly fruit and smaller, nonsticky, winter buds.

Leaves Compound, with 5 to 7 leaflets radiating from the same point on the leafstalk. Each leaflet, to 20 cm long and 10 cm broad, is pointed and has prominent parallel veins. They turn from bright green to orange or yellow in autumn.

Bark Dark reddish-brown or grey-brown, breaking away in large shallow plates.

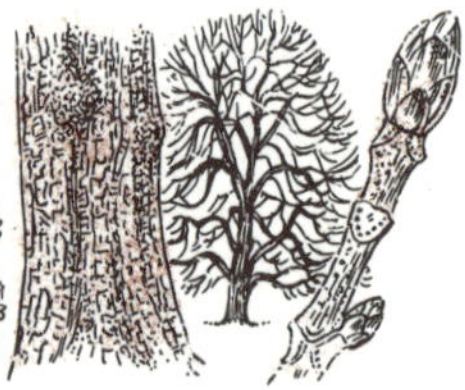

Winter buds and twigs Pointed red-brown buds, 2.5 cm long and 1.5 cm broad, become sticky in early spring. The twigs have distinctive leaf scars shaped like horseshoes.

Description A massive deciduous tree, to 30 m or more, with a tall domed crown on a short stout trunk. Its upright clusters of white flowers are distinctive in early summer and its fruits and seeds (conkers) in autumn; in winter the tree can be recognized by its large sticky winter buds.

Habitat Parks, gardens, squares and greens, where it is planted for ornament.
Range Introduced from Greece and Albania; common and widespread.
Annual cycle Leaves: May-November; flowers: May-June; fruit: August-November.

Common lime *Tilia* × *europaea; T.* × *vulgaris*

TILIACEAE

Fruit Globular or egg-shaped, 8 mm across, with a buff-coloured slightly ribbed and downy surface. They are borne in clusters like the flowers.

Large-leaved lime (*T. platyphyllos*). It differs from the common lime in its larger leaves (to 15 cm), which are hairy on both surfaces; its ribbed and very downy fruits; and the absence of shoots and bosses on the trunk.

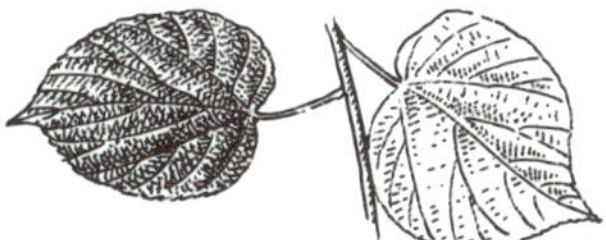

Leaves Heart-shaped, 6-10 cm long (larger on the side stems), with a lopsided base and toothed margins. They are dull green above and paler beneath with tufts of hair at the bases of the veins.

Flowers Yellowish-white and sweet-scented, borne in drooping clusters of 4 to 10 attached to a slender yellowish-green leaflike bract.

Winter buds Reddish-brown and egg-shaped, with two outer scales, one larger than the other.

Bark Smooth and dull grey, becoming rough and cracked into a network of ridges in old trees.

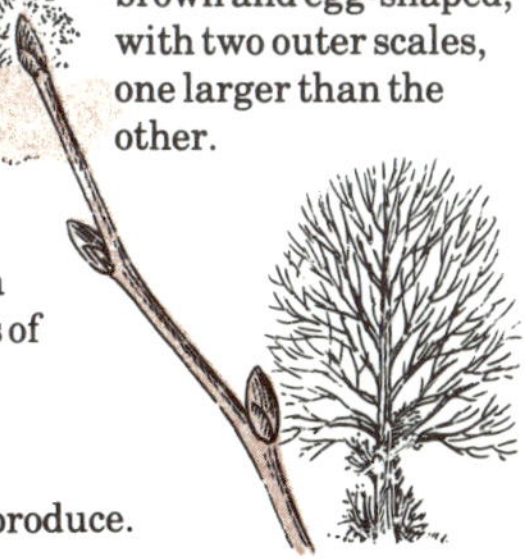

Description A large deciduous tree, to 40 m with a tall domed crown. A distinctive feature at all times of the year is the presence of numerous bushy side stems and bosses near the base of the trunk. In summer the tree is attacked by greenfly and the ground beneath is sticky with the honeydew they produce.

Habitat Streets, avenues, parks, churchyards, etc., where it is planted for ornament and shade.
Range N.W. Europe; very common and widespread.
Annual cycle Leaves: May-October; flowers: June-July; fruit: August-October.

Elder *Sambucus nigra*

CAPRIFOLIACEAE

Leaves Compound, with 5 to 7 leaflets set in pairs on either side of the stalk with a single leaflet at the tip. Each leaflet is oval, to 8 cm long, with a pointed tip and toothed margins. They change from dark green to yellow in autumn.

Fruit A berry, about 5 mm across, grouped in clusters and ripening from green to blue-black.

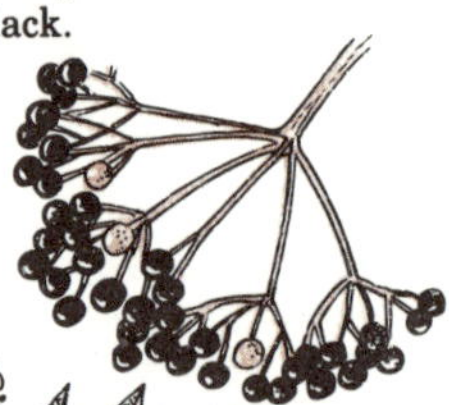

Bark Thick, corky, greyish-brown, and deeply furrowed.

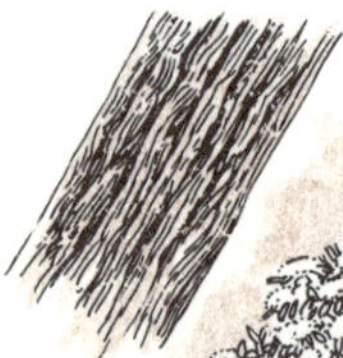

Flowers Creamy-white, about 5 mm across, borne in flat-topped clusters 10-20 cm across. They (and the berries) are used for making wine.

Description A deciduous shrub or small tree, to 10 m, with an irregular much-branched crown. Its clusters of creamy-white flowers and blue-black berries in summer are distinctive features, as are its scaleless buds in winter.

Winter buds Purplish-brown tufts, lacking scales, set in pairs on the twig.

Habitat Grows wild in woods, hedgerows, scrub and wasteland.
Range Europe, N. Africa and W. Asia; common and widespread.
Annual cycle Leaves: April-October; flowers: June-July; fruit: August-September.

OLEACEAE

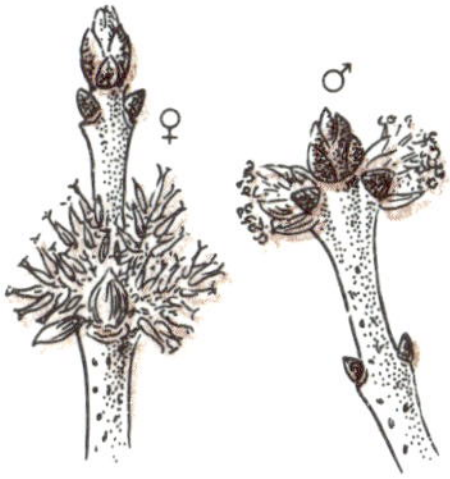

Fruit A slender wing, 4 cm long, with a seed at the base. Wings hang in drooping clusters and ripen from green to brown.

Leaves Compound, with 9 to 13 leaflets arranged in pairs on the stalk with a single leaflet at the tip. Each leaflet is dull green, slender and pointed, to 12 cm, with forward-pointing teeth and hairs on the undersurface.

Flowers Tiny male, female and hermaphrodite (both sexes) flowers may all be seen on the same tree. They appear before the leaves and grow in tight clusters, the male flowers purple then yellow with pollen, the females purple and green.

Bark Pale grey, with a network of shallow rides, becoming thick in old trees.

Winter buds Small, pointed and black, set in pairs on the twig with three at the twig tip.

Description A tall deciduous tree, to 42 m, with a tall-domed crown of branches that ascend almost vertically from the trunk. It is easily recognized in winter by its black winter buds on smooth pale grey twigs and by its distinctive fruits.

Habitat Grows wild forming woods in alkaline soils; also planted in parks, churchyards, etc.
Range Europe and S.W. Asia; common and widespread.
Annual cycle Flowers: April-May; leaves: May-October; fruit: July-December.

Practical 1 – Keeping records

An essential part of the study of trees is keeping detailed and accurate records of your findings. Not only will this make it much easier for you to identify trees of the same species when you come across them in the future, but it will also help to make you aware of trees as living things that undergo a regular (usually annual) cycle of growth and reproduction. This is reflected in the changes that are apparent in the trees' appearance throughout the year.

Equipment required

1. Notebook, pens and pencils. These are essential for making notes, sketches and drawings of your finds.
2. A hand lens or magnifying glass, for examining the detailed structure of buds, flowers, leaves, etc.
3. A camera. This is optional, but photographs often convey a more realistic picture than sketches, especially of whole trees. The camera should be capable of taking standard and close-up shots.
4. Ruler, tape measure and string. All these are essential measuring tools. You will need the string for dimensions greater than those covered by normal tape measures.
5. Polythene bags, jars or similar containers, and water. These are for storing specimens. Some parts of trees (e.g. leaves and flowers) may need to be stored in water to prevent wilting.

What to record

1. **Evidence of identity** The first thing to do is identify the tree(s) you are studying, using the keys and ready reference sections in the front section of this book. The key you use will depend on which parts of the tree are available, which is determined by the season. The record should start with the date and the species name of the tree.
2. **Location** It is important to note the location of your tree (a wood, park, field, etc.) and to describe the surroundings in which it is growing. A particular point to note is whether the tree is growing in the open or crowded together with other trees: this will affect its height and the shape of its crown.
3. **Parts of the tree** Note the size, colour and other descriptive features of any parts that are available. Use sketches or photographs to supplement the description. You may wish to collect specimens of leaves, fruits, buds, etc. (Methods of preserving these are described in Practical 2 and Practical 3, pp. 74-77.)
4. **Height** There is a simple method of estimating the height of a tree using a stick, tape measure and string.

Holding your arm straight in front of you with the fist clenched, measure the distance from your eye to the tip of your clasping fingers. Cut a stick of exactly this length.

Holding the stick straight in front of you at its middle, face the tree and walk backwards, using one eye to align the tree with the stick until the tip and base of the tree are exactly in line with the top and bottom of the stick.

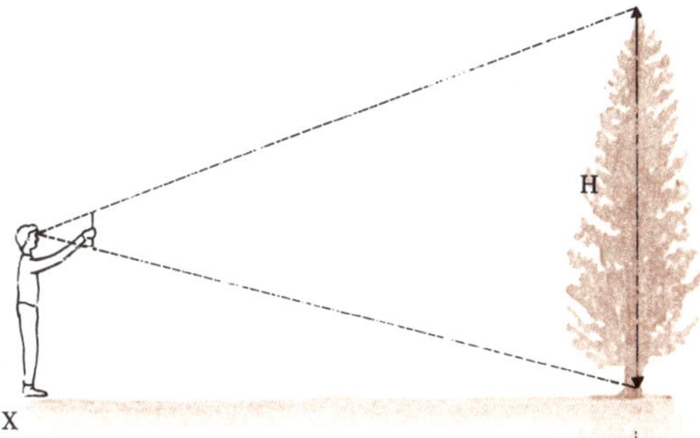

Mark your position on the ground (X) when the tree is aligned and measure the distance between this point and the centre of the base of the tree. This distance (D) will give you the height of the tree (H), the two measurements being equal.

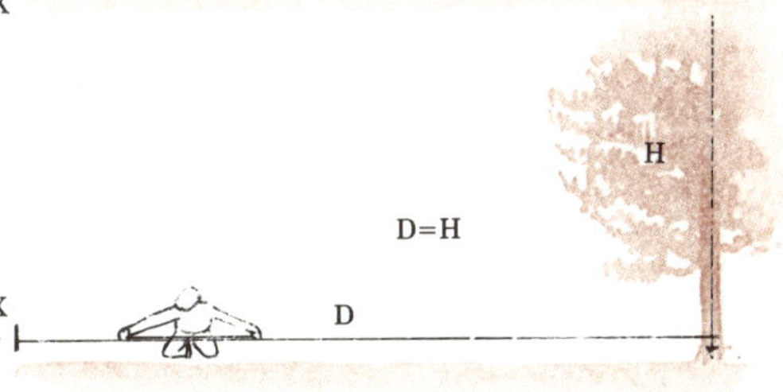

5. **Age** A very simple method of estimating the age of a tree can be carried out using only a tape measure or piece of string. It is based on the fact that most trees increase in girth by 2.5 cm a year. Note, however, that this method will only work for mature trees growing in the open and not crowded by others nearby. In addition, it will not work for very young or very old trees, or for a few species with growth rates faster or slower than the average.

Using the tape measure or string, measure the girth of the tree at a point 1.5 m from the highest point of the surrounding ground. Dividing the girth measurement by 2.5 cm will give the approximate age of the tree. Thus a tree with a girth of 2.5 m would be about 100 years old (i.e. 250 cm ÷ 2.5 cm).

Suggestions for projects

1. Select a particular tree in your area for a long-term study and record the changes it undergoes throughout the year. Take photographs or make drawings of leaves, flowers, twigs etc. at monthly intervals or when appropriate. If the tree is deciduous, note when the leaves appear; observe changes in the colour, texture and size of the leaves until they fall. Note when the flowers open and when the fruits start forming. If the tree is a conifer, follow the development of the cones; some cones take more than one year to ripen.
2. Select a habitat for study, such as a wood or park, and record all the trees and shrubs in a sample section of it. You can do this for a particular season or throughout the year. If you are studying a wood, see if one species of tree is more prevalent than all the others or if two or more species are equally common.

Practical 2 – Preserving material

There are various ways in which parts of trees can be preserved. However, since most of these methods result in some change in the colour or appearance of the specimen, it is advisable to take drawings or photographs of the material before you preserve it. These can then be used to supplement the preserved specimens when you compile a full record of the tree(s) you are studying (see Practical 1, p. 72-73).

Natural drying

This method is suitable for hard, dry specimens, such as cones, nuts, some evergreen leaves (especially the leaf sprays of Lawson's and Leyland's cypresses), pieces of bark that have become detached from the tree, and twigs with winter buds. Remove any earth or other debris from your specimen and, if wet, leave it to dry off. Leaves should be placed on paper and dried away from the light to preserve their colour. Bark and winter buds may be coated with a clear varnish.

Pressing

This method is best for leaves and flat, dry fruits (e.g. sycamore wings and ash keys). It can also be used for flowers, although pressing inevitably distorts their natural structure.

Place your specimen between two sheets of blotting paper. If you are pressing flowers make sure that the petals do not become folded or displaced when you do this. Insert the blotting paper with its specimen between the pages of a large heavy book (an old telephone directory is ideal), and place some more books on top of this. Leave for a week and then remove the specimen, but handle it carefully so that you do not damage it (use tweezers for small leaves and flowers).

Glycerine method

This is a method for preserving leaves that retains their natural shape and texture. Most leaves preserved in this way change colour, usually to a darker shade of their original colour. The process involves the leaves drawing up a glycerine solution in the same way that they would normally draw up water. *Equipment required* (1) A screw-top jar. (2) A glass or plastic beaker. (3) Glycerine. (4) Hot water.

1. Pour glycerine into the screw-top jar until it is one-third full. Then fill the jar with hot water, screw on the top and shake until the glycerine and water are thoroughly mixed and the liquid is clear. Pour this mixture into the glass or beaker to a depth of about 5 cm.

2. Evergreen leaves can be collected at any time of the year, but deciduous leaves are best preserved when they are mature, between July and September. Select a twig with one or more leaves attached. Place your twigs in the glycerine mixture as soon as they are picked and stand the glass in a cool dry dark place.

3. Preserving time varies with the size and thickness of the leaf. Thin leaves will be ready in 2-3 days, while tough leathery ones may require several weeks. The process is complete when the entire leaf has changed colour. The preserved leaf is best stored in a closed box.

Borax method

This is a method for drying flowers in which their natural shape and colour are maintained. It is not suitable for flowers with large, fragile petals.

Equipment required (1) Borax. (2) A shallow tray, such as an old baking tray. (3) A cardboard box; an old shoe or stationery box is good for this purpose. (4) A sieve. (5) A small paintbrush.

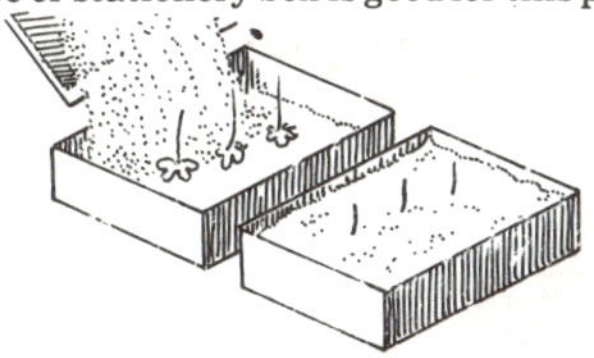

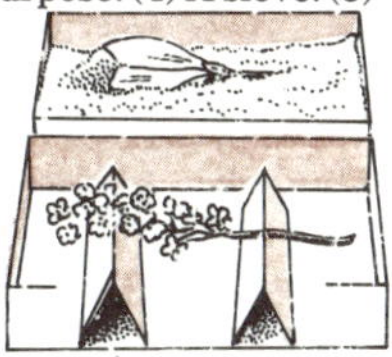

1. Spread the borax evenly over the surface of the tray and leave in a warm dry place (such as an airing cupboard) until completely dry.

2. Fill the box with dried borax to a depth of 2.5 cm. Place your flowers in it and sieve more borax onto them until they are completely covered. Take care not to damage the petals. Some flowers may need to be supported on struts. Cup-shaped flowers should be filled, as well as covered, with borax.

3. Place the box in a warm, dry place and leave for 1-5 days, depending on the size and thickness of the petals. Test if a flower is dry by holding it to your ear and flicking it gently: it should sound papery.

4. Leave the dried flowers at room temperature for a few hours, then carefully remove any excess borax with the paintbrush. Flowers preserved in this way should then be kept in a dry atmosphere away from direct light.

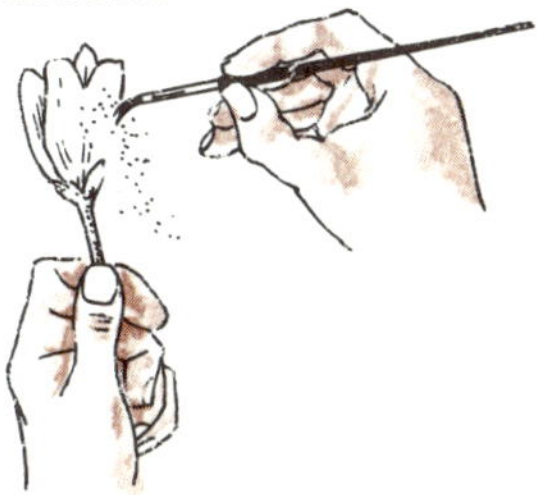

You will find that some tree parts are not suitable for any of the preserving methods described in Practical 2, pp. 74-75. Two methods of making permanent records of such material are described below.

Plaster casts

This method is suitable for winter twigs, leaves, bark and hard fruits. *Equipment required* (1) Plasticine or modelling clay. (2) Sheets of plain paper. (3) A wooden block or any other firm flat object, such as a hardback book. (4) Long strips of cardboard or stiff paper, 3-5 cm wide. (5) Paper clips. (6) Plaster of Paris. (7) Water. (8) A container and stick for mixing the plaster. (9) A knife. (10) Poster paints and paintbrush.

Making the mould. Shape the plasticine into a flat rectangle 2 cm deep and 2-3 cm longer and wider than the specimen. Place a sheet of paper over the top surface of the plasticine and press with the wooden block until the surface is flat.

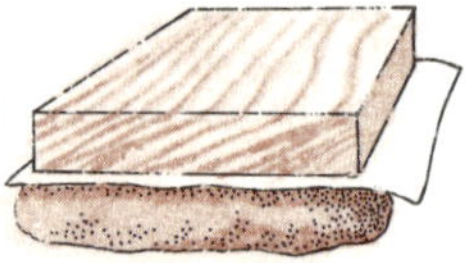

For twigs and spherical or egg-shaped fruits, press the specimen firmly into the plasticine with the wooden block until you have a distinct, well-formed mould.

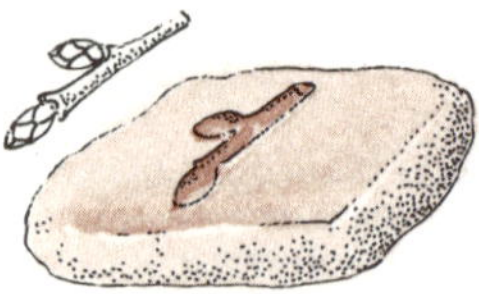

For leaves and flat fruits, place a sheet of paper over the specimen and press with the wooden block until a clear impression of the specimen is made in the plasticine.

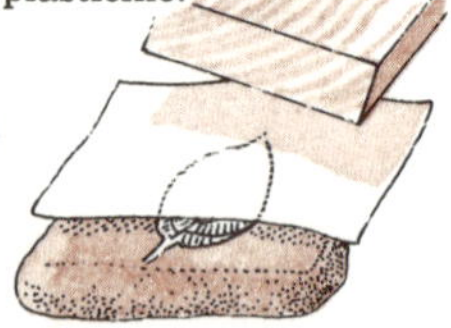

For bark moulds, shape a rectangle of plasticine 2 cm thick to a size that will show all the important features of the bark, say 8 cm long and 5 cm wide. Place the plasticine on the tree trunk and press firmly.

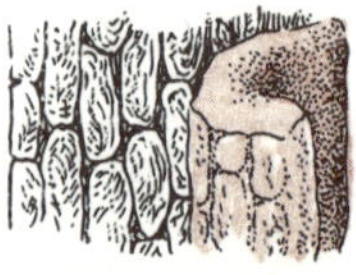

Making the cast Place a strip of cardboard around the mould and secure with a paper clip.

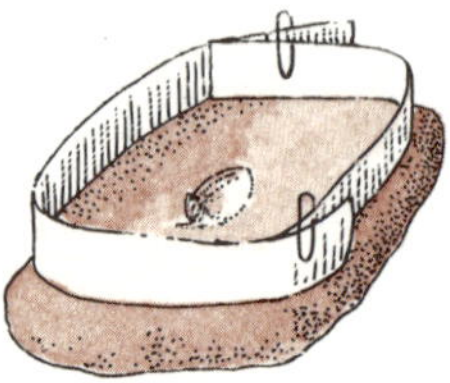

Put some water in the container and add plaster of Paris a little at a time, stirring continuously until you have a thick creamy mixture.

Pour this mixture into the mould to a depth of about 2 cm.

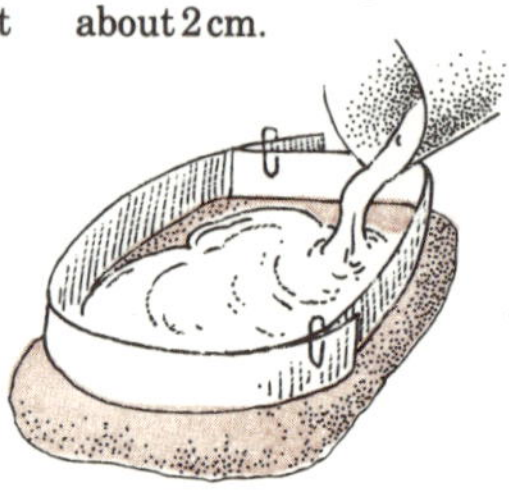

When the plaster is cold, remove the cardboard and carefully peel off the plasticine (and paper) with a knife.

When the cast is completely dry, paint in the details with poster paint, referring to the original specimen.

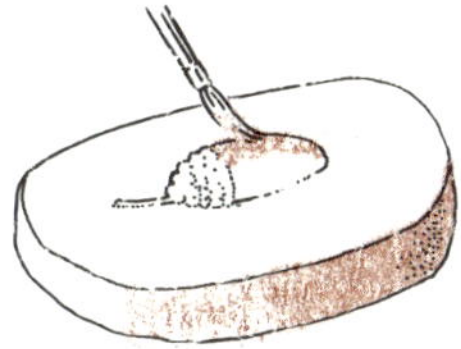

Scribble prints

Prints may be made of leaves, flat fruits, and bark.

Equipment required (1) Plain white paper. (2) Coloured wax crayons. (3) A black lead pencil.

For leaves and fruits, place the specimen (underside upwards for leaves) on a flat surface and cover with plain paper.

Using a crayon the same colour as the specimen, scribble gently over it until all the details show clearly.

Draw in the outline of the specimen with the black pencil.

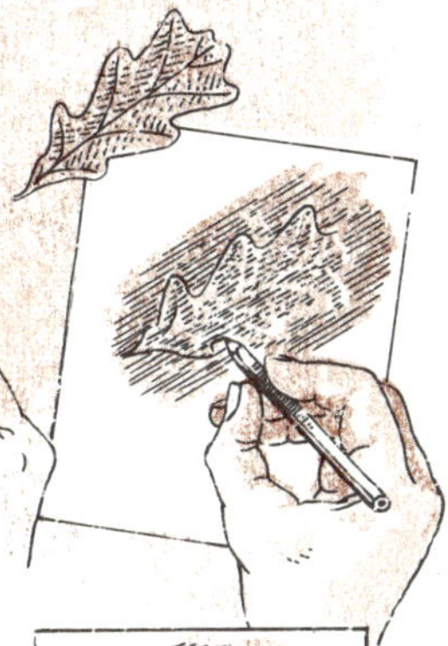

For bark, place the paper over the surface of the tree trunk.

Scribble gently over the surface with a crayon the same colour as the bark.

The sites listed below contain good specimens of both common and rarer trees. Never pick leaves or other parts from trees growing in gardens: either study the parts *in situ* or collect specimens that have fallen to the ground.

England
Waddesdon House, Aylesbury, Buckinghamshire
Cambridge Botanic Garden
Glendurgan, Falmouth, Cornwall
Bicton, East Budleigh, Devon
Epping Forest, Essex
Hatfield Forest, Essex
Forest of Dean, Gloucestershire
Westonbirt Arboretum, Nr. Tetbury, Gloucestershire
New Forest, Hampshire
National Pinetum, Bedgebury, Kent
Hyde Park and Kensington Gardens, London
Royal Botanic Gardens, Kew, Surrey
Royal Horticultural Society's Gardens, Wisley, Ripley, Surrey
Ashdown Forest, Sussex
Wakehurst Place, Ardingly, Sussex
Studley Royal and Fountains Abbey, Nr. Ripon, Yorkshire
Liverpool University Botanic Gardens, Liverpool
Chatsworth House, Derbyshire
Harlow Car Gardens, Harrogate, Yorkshire

Wales
Roath Park, Cardiff
Bodnant, Tal-y-Cefn, Conway, Gwynedd
Vivod Forest Garden, Llangollen, Clwyd

Scotland
Brodick Castle, Arran
Royal Botanic Garden, Edinburgh
Moniac Glen, Nr. Beauly, Highland Region
Scone Palace, Nr. Perth
Culzean Castle, Girvan, Strathclyde Region
Inveraray Castle Gardens, Strathclyde Region

Ireland
Castlewellan, Newcastle, Co. Down
Birr Castle, Co. Offaly
John F. Kennedy Memorial Arboretum, New Ross, Co. Wexford
Powerscourt, Co. Wicklow

The titles listed below deal with more species than has been possible in this book:

Mitchell, A. (1974) *A Field Guide to the Trees of Britain and Northern Europe*, Collins
Mitchell, A. and Wilkinson, J. (1982) *The Trees of Britain and Northern Europe*, Collins
Nicholson, B. E. and Clapham, A. R. (1975) *The Oxford Book of Trees*, Oxford University Press
Polunin, O. and Everard, B. (1976) *Trees and Bushes of Europe*, Oxford University Press
Phillips, R. (1978) *Trees in Britain*, Pan Books

Glossary

Boss: Rounded knobbly growth on some tree trunks.
Bract: Leaf-like structure. In lime trees flowers grow from bracts.
Carpel: Female organ of a flower, bearing the stigma.
Catkin: Cluster of very small stalkless flowers, often hanging down.
Compound leaf: Leaf made up of three or more leaflets growing from the same stalk.
Crown: Branches and leaves of a tree, as distinct from the trunk.
Deciduous tree: Tree shedding all its leaves at the same time of the year, having bare branches in winter.
Evergreen: Tree that sheds and replaces its leaves continuously, never having bare branches.
Fluted: Having rounded grooves in the trunk running from top to bottom.
Gall: Rounded lump on leaves or other parts, usually caused by insects.
Hermaphrodite: Having both male and female reproductive organs.
Hybrid: Tree resulting from a cross between two trees of different species.
Introduced: Brought in from another country; not native.
Leaflet: Small leaf, several of which make up a compound leaf.
Midrib: Largest vein of a leaf, usually running from base to tip.
Naturalized: Adapted to growing in the wild after having been introduced from another country.
Nutlet: Small dry fruit containing a single seed, as seen in sycamore.
Pollen: Mass of tiny yellow grains containing male sex cells, produced by the stamens.
Species: Group of similar trees that interbreed naturally.
Spur: A short section of a branchlet (a small branch) usually bearing a cluster of leaves.
Stamen: Male organ of a flower, producing pollen.
Stigma: Part of the female organ of a flower on which pollen is deposited.
Sucker: Shoot arising from a root or stem below ground and eventually growing into a new tree.
Winter bud: Bud present on a tree throughout winter that grows into a new shoot the following spring.

Acacia, false 14, 22, 64
Alder, common 10-13, 14, 23, 44
Almond 14, 23, 58
Apple 9
  Crab 6, 14, 23, 56
Ash 9, 10-13, 22, 23
  Common 71
  Mountain *see* Rowan
Aspen 14, 23, 39
Beech, common 14, 15, 22, 23, 48
Birch, silver 10-13, 22, 23, 45
Blackthorn 11-13, 23, 59
Cedar 14
  Atlas 28
  of Lebanon 22, 28
Cherry 9, 14, 22, 23
  Japanese 'Kanzan' flowering 23, 58
  Wild 57
Chestnut
  Horse 14, 23, 68
  Red horse 68
  Sweet 14, 22, 23 49
Christmas *see* Spruce, Norway
Cypress
  Lawson's 14, 22, 35
  Leyland 14, 35
Deodar 28
Elder 14, 23, 70
Elm
  Smooth-leaved 52
  Wych 10-13, 23, 52
Fir
  Douglas 14, 22, 32
  Grand 14, 22, 27
Gean *see* Cherry, wild
Hawthorn 11-13, 23, 55
Hazel 9, 10-13, 23, 47
Hemlock, western 14, 22, 23
Holly 10-13, 23, 65
Hornbeam 14, 22, 23, 46
Juniper 14, 22, 36
Laburnum 14, 22, 23, 63
Larch, european 9, 14, 22, 29
Lime
  Common 14, 22, 23, 69
  Large-leaved 69
Locust *see* Acacia, false
Magnolia, soulange 14, 23, 53
Maple, Norway 23, 67
Monkey puzzle 14, 38
Oak 9, 10-13
  Durmast *see* Oak, sessile
  English 22, 23, 50
  Holly *see* Oak, holm
  Holm 14, 51
  Pendunulate *see* Oak, English
  Sessile 50
Pear 14, 23, 60
Pine 9
  Chile *see* Monkey puzzle
  Corsican 14, 31
  Scots 14, 22, 31
Plane, London 9, 14, 22, 23, 54
Poplar
  Black 40
  Lombardy 14, 22, 23, 40
  White 39
Redwood, coast 14, 22, 34
Robinia *see* Acacia, false
Rowan 11-13, 23, 61
Sallow *see* Willow, goat
Sloe *see* Blackthorn
Spindle 14, 23, 66
Spruce
  Norway 6, 14, 22, 30
  Sitka 30
Sycamore 9, 10-13, 23, 67
Walnut 14, 23, 43
Whitebeam 14, 23, 62
Willow
  Crack 14, 23, 41
  Goat 10-13, 14, 23, 42
  Pussy *see* Willow, weeping
  Weeping 14, 22, 41
Yew
  Common 14, 22, 37
  Irish 37